Danish Contributions to Classical Scholarship

Danish Humanist Texts and Studies

Volume 27

Edited by Erland Kolding Nielsen

The Royal Library Copenhagen

Danish Contributions to Classical Scholarship
1971-1991
A Bibliography

by
Flemming Gorm Andersen

THE ROYAL LIBRARY, COPENHAGEN
MUSEUM TUSCULANUM PRESS
2004

Danish Contributions to Classical Scholarship
© 2004, The Royal Library, Copenhagen, and Museum Tusculanum Press
Set and printed in Denmark by Special-Trykkeriet Viborg a-s
Paper: Book Design Smooth, 100 g
The paper meets the requirements of ISO 9706: 1994
ISBN 87 7289 822 4
ISSN 0105 8746

Published with the support from
The Danish Research Council for the Humanities

Museum Tusculanum Press
Njalsgade 94
DK-2300 Copenhagen S
www.mtp.dk

TABLE OF CONTENTS

Preface	9
Acknowledgements	10
List of abbreviations	11
Introduction	16
Authors and texts (1-288)	19
Epigraphy	51
Minoan and Mycenaean epigraphy (289-301)	51
Greek epigraphy (302-318)	52
Latin epigraphy (319-322)	54
Papyrology (323-348)	54
Palaeography and textual criticism (349-353)	57
Manuscripts in Denmark (354)	58
Language (355)	58
Greek language (356-357)	58
Greek etymology and lexicography (358-362)	58
Greek phonology and inflexion (363-364)	59
Greek syntax (365-366)	59
Latin language	59
Latin etymology and lexicography (367-378)	59
Latin phonology and inflexion (379)	61
History of literature (380-385)	61
History of Greek literature (386-391)	61
History of Latin literature (392-399)	62
History	63
General, political, and legal history (400)	63
Social, economic, and cultural history (401-403)	63
Greek history	63
Greek general, political, and legal history (404-405)	63
Greek socal, economic, and cultural history (406-407)	64
Etruscan history (408-416)	64
Roman history	65
Roman general and political history (417-423)	65
Roman constitutional and administrative history (424-429)	65
Roman social, economic, and cultural history (430-440)	66

Roman social, economic, and cultural history (430-440)	66
Biography (441-442)	67
Topography	67
Greece (443-613)	68
Italy and Sicily (614-693)	85
Europe outside Greece and Italy (694-701)	92
Asia Minor (702-733)	93
Cyprus (734-741)	96
Syria and Palestine (742-762)	96
Other areas of Asia (763-770)	100
Africa (771-786)	101
Art and archaeology (787-793)	103
Greek (incl. Prehistoric) art and archaeology (794-803)	103
Etruscan and Italic art and archaeology (804-820)	105
Roman art and archaeology (821-828)	106
Architecture	107
Greek (incl. Prehistoric) architecture (829-832)	107
Etruscan and Italic architecture (833-834)	107
Roman architecture (835-840)	108
Sculpture (841-842)	108
Greek sculpture (843-862)	109
Etruscan sculpture (863-869)	110
Roman sculpture (870-899)	111
Pottery (900-951)	114
Terracottas, ivories (952-960)	119
Gems and sealings (961-970)	120
Bronzes, Other metalwork, and glass (971-993)	121
Numismatics (994-995)	123
Greek numismatics (996-1064)	123
Roman numismatics (1065-1070)	129
Danish museums (1071-1074)	130
The National Museum (1075-1082)	131
The Ny Carlsberg Glyptothek (1083-1090)	132
Thorvaldsen's Museum (1091)	133
Religion and mythology (1092-1099)	133
Greek religion and mythology (1100-1106)	134
Roman religion and mythology (1107-1113)	135
Philosophy (1114-1141)	135

Science and technology (1142-1143) 139
   Mathematics, astronomy (1144-1156) 139
   Medicine (1157-1159) 140
   Technology (1160-1171) 141
History of Danish classical scholarship (1172-1174) 142
Generalia et collectanea (1175-1183) 142

Index annorum 144
Index of authors 148

PREFACE

For generations, The Royal Library has contributed to or published bibliographies of the major subjects, especially within the field of humanities and social sciences. One of these is the present bibliography of Classical studies.

For many years, Classical studies in Denmark have been covered by two parallel bibliographies, which comprise Danish and foreign language literature respectively. A current total of six volumes register practically everything published from the 16th century until 1991. Three of these volumes have been published in The Royal Library's series *Danish Humanist Texts and Studies*. With *Danish Contributions to Classical Scholarship 1971-1991*, the bibliography of publications in foreign languages have been brought into line with the Danish-language *Danmark og Antikken* of which the latest volume covering the years 1980-1991 was published in 1994. Research librarian Flemming Gorm Andersen, subject specialist on Classical and Near Eastern Antiquity at the Royal Library, has compiled both.

Though the bibliography is based on a database, it is initially published as a printed work. This may appear somewhat old-fashioned. But while a *database* is, of course, an unsurpassed research tool for rapid retrieval of specific titles or subjects, a *printed version* offers other possibilities of orientation and a systematic, comparative view. Some bibliographies are still made to be *read* – an aspect sometimes overlooked today.

From 1992 onwards, however, the two series of the classical bibliography will be integrated, irrespective of language, and published as a database. Furthermore, depending on the financial circumstances, the future plan is to retroconvert the printed bibliographies for a combined subject database.

On behalf of The Royal Library, I extend my warm thanks to the State Research Council for the Humanities for financial support for the printing of the bibliography.

The Royal Library, March 2004
Erland Kolding Nielsen, Director

ACKNOWLEDGEMENTS

While preparing this bibliography, I have acquired several pleasant debts of gratitude.

To Director General Erland Kolding Nielsen, The Royal Library, for continuous support as well as for the acceptance of the result for Danish Humanist Texts and Studies.

To my colleagues at The Royal Library for advice and assistance.

To all those scholars who have checked and supplemented my information, answered numerous additional questions, and patiently waited for the result to appear.

To the staff at Museum Tusculanum Press for unstinted help and co-operation – with special thanks to John Roberts for his check of style and spelling.

Last, but not least, to The Danish Research Council for the Humanities, and to The Royal Library, for grants to cover the publication costs.

My heartfelt thanks to them all. Such shortcomings as may still remain, are entirely my own.

Flemming Gorm Andersen

ABBREVIATIONS

AA	Archäologischer Anzeiger
AAA	'Αρχαιολογικα 'Ανάλεκτα εζ 'Αθηνον
AArch	Acta archaeologica
AC	Archeologia Classica
ActaAArtHist	Acta ad archaeologiam et artium historiam pertinentia
ActaArchHung	Acta archaeologica Academiae scientiarum Hungaricae
ActaSLU	Acta Societatis linguisticae Upsaliensis, Nova Series
ADAJ	Annual of the Department of Antiquities of Jordan
ADelt	'Αρχαιολογικον Δελτίον
AEphem	'Αρχαιολογικη 'Εφημερίς
AGPh	Archiv für Geschichte der Philosophie
AGR	Akten der Gesellschaft für griechische und römische Rechtsgeschichte
AHB	The Ancient History Bulletin
AIHS	Archives internationales d'histoire des sciences
AIIN	Annali Istituto italiano di numismatica
AJA	American Journal of Archaeology
AJAH	American Journal of Ancient History
AJPh	American Journal of Philology
AncW	The Ancient World
AnnPerugia	Annali della Facoltà di lettere e filosofia, Università degli studi di Perugia
ANRW	Aufstieg und Niedergang der römischen Welt
ANSMN	American Numismatic Society Museum Notes
AR	Archaeological Reports
ArchLaz	Archeologia Laziale
ArchViva	Archeologica Viva
ARID	Analecta Romana Instituti Danici
ARV	ARV. Scandinavian Yearbook of Folklore
BABesch	Bulletin Antieke beschaving
BCH	Bulletin de correspondance hellénique
BdA	Bollettino d'Arte
BerOudBod	Berichten van de Rijksdienst voor het Oudheidkundig

	Bodemonderzoek
BiblArch	Biblical Archaeologist
BibO	Bibliotheca Orientalis
BICS	Bulletin of the Institute of Classical Studies of the University of London
BJb	Bonner Jahrbücher des rheinischen Landesmuseums in Bonn
BSA	The Annual of the British School at Athens
BullCom	Bullettino della Comissione archeologica comunale di Roma
BZ	Byzantinische Zeitschrift
C&M	Classica et mediaevalia
CahEtAnc	Cahiers des études anciennes
CEDAC	Centre d'études et de documentation archéologique de la Conservation de Carthage. Bulletin
CEFR	Collection de l'École française à Rome
ChrÉg	Chronique d'Égypte
CIMAGL	Cahiers de l'institut du moyen âge grec et latin
CoinH	Coin Hoards
CP	Classical Philology
CQ	The Classical Quarterly
CR	The Classical Review
CretSt	Cretan Studies
CronErcol	Cronache ercolanesi
CW	The Classical World
DOAI	Juul Kristensen, B. & Majlund Kristensen, J.: Danmark og antikken 1968-1979 (= Antikken i Danmark 2). Kbh., 1982.
DOAII	Andersen, F.G.: Danmark og antikken 1980-1991 (= Danish Humanist Texts and Studies 8). Kbh., 1994.
DTT	Dansk Teologisk Tidsskrift
DYPhilos	Danish Yearbook of Philosophy
EAA	Enciclopedia dell'Arte Antica Classica e Orientale
FilRUCPrep	Filosofi og videnskabsteori på Roskilde Universitetscenter. 3. Række: Preprints og reprints
FMS	Frühmittelalterliche Studien
GettyMusJ	The J. Paul Getty Museum Journal
GRBS	Greek, Roman and Byzantine Studies

HistFilolMed	Historisk-filologiske meddelelser / Det Kongelige Danske Videnskabernes Selskab
HistFilosMed	Historisk-filosofiske meddelelser / Det Kongelige Danske Videnskabernes Selskab
HistFilosSkr	Historisk-filosofiske skrifter / Det Kongelige Danske Videnskabernes Selskab
HM	Historia mathematica. International journal of the history of mathematics
HSF	Historische Sprachforschung
HT	Historisk tidsskrift (København)
HTech	History of Technology
ICS	Illinois Classical Studies
IJNA	The International Journal of Nautical Archaeology and Underwater Exploration
INJ	Israel Numismatic Journal
IstMitt	Istanbuler Mitteilungen
JAC	Jahrbuch für Antike und Christentum
JAS	Journal of Archaeological Science
JdI	Jahrbuch des Deutschen Archäologischen Instituts
JEA	The Journal of Egyptian Archaeology
JFA	Journal of Field Archaeology
JHA	Journal for the History of Astronomy
JHPh	Journal of the History of Philosophy
JHS	The Journal of Hellenic Studies
JNG	Jahrbuch für Numismatik und Geldgeschichte
JRA	Journal of Roman Archaeology
JRS	The Journal of Roman Studies
JSJ	Journal for the Study of Judaism
JSP	Journal for the Study of the Pseudepigrapha
KölnJb	Kölner Jahrbuch für Vor- und Frühgeschichte
LCM	Liverpool Classical Monthly
LingBibl	Linguistica biblica
MBeitr	Madrider Beiträge
MededRom	Mededelingen van het Nederlands Historisch Instituut te Rome
Medusa	Medusa. Svensk tidskrift för antiken (Stockholm)
MH	Museum Helveticum
MittLeichtweiss	Mitteilungen d. Leichtweiss-Institut für Wasserbau

Mosaic	Mosaic. Journal of the Comparative Study of International Literature, Art and Ideas. New Delhi.
MT	Museum Tusculanum
MZ	Mainzer Zeitschrift
NAC	Numismatica e antichità classiche. Quaderni Ticinesi
NachrAkGött	Nachrichten der Akademie der Wissenschaften in Göttingen. Philologisch-Historische Klasse
NC	Numismatic Chronicle
NNÅ	Nordisk Numismatisk Årsskrift
NotMilano	Notizie dal Chiostro del Manastero maggiore. Rassegna di studi del Civico museo archeologico ... di Milano
NordJud	Nordisk Judaistik = Scandinavian Jewish Studies (Stockholm)
NSc	Notizie degli scavi di antichità
OpAth	Opuscula Atheniensia
OpRom	Opuscula Romana
PAH	Hansen, P.A.: A Bibliography of Danish Contributions to Classical Scholarship from the Sixteenth Centrury to 1970 (= Danish Humanist Texts and Studies 1). Kbh., 1977.
PEQ	Palestine Exploration Quarterly
PhR	Philosophical Review
Polhem	Polhem. Tidsskrift för teknikhistoria (Stockholm)
PP	La parola del passato
QArchEtr	Quaderni del Centro di studio per l'archeologia etrusco-italica
QUCC	Quaderni urbinati di cultura classica
RA	Revue archéologique
RDAC	Report of the Department of Antiquities, Cyprus
REA	Revue des Études anciennes
RhM	Rheinisches Museum für Philologie
RHT	Revue d'histoire des textes
RIN	Rivista italiana di numismatica e scienze affini
RMeta	The Review of Metaphysics
SIMA	Studies in Mediterranean Archaeology
SkrAth	Skrifter utgivna av Svenska Institutet i Athen
SkrRom	Skrifter utgivna av Svenska Institutet i Rom
SMEA	Studi micenei ed egeo-anatolici

SNR	Schweizerische numismatische Rundschau
StClas	Studii clasice
StEtr	Studi etruschi
STh	Scandinavian Journal of Theology
StHell	Studia Hellenistica
SymbOsl	Symbolae osloenses
T&C	Technology and Culture
TLL	Thesaurus Linguae Latinae
TribArq	Tribunal d'Arquelogia (Barcelona)
WJA	Würzburger Jahrbücher für die Altertumswissenschaft
WS	Wiener Studien
WZBerlin	Wissenschaftliche Zeitschrift der Humboldt-Universität zu Berlin
ZfdA	Zeitschrift für deutsches Altertum und deutsche Literatur
ŽivaAnt	Živa antika. Antiquité vivante
ZPE	Zeitschrift für Papyrologie und Epigraphik
ZWG	Sudhoffs Archiv. Zeitschrift für Wissenschaftsgeschichte
ZÄS	Zeitschrift für ägyptische Sprache und Altertumskunde

INTRODUCTION

The present volume is a continuation of P.A. Hansen's *Bibliography of Danish Contributions to Classical Scholarship from the Sixteenth Century to 1970* (Copenhagen 1977), continuing the registration up to 1991. The chronological limit was chosen so as to fit the bibliographies of classical studies in Danish, comprising four separate books (Chr. Thaarup: *Fortegnelse paa danske Oversættelser af græske og latinske Skribenter* (2. ed., 1836); K. Elkjær & P. Krarup: *Danmark og Antiken* (2. ed., 1968); B.J. Kristensen & J.M. Kristensen: *Danmark og antikken 1968-1979* (1982); F.G. Andersen: *Danmark og antikken 1980-1991* (1994)). Though the aim and selection criteria of the six volumes differ somewhat, they constitute a practically complete documentation of Danish classical studies through 420 years.

As a continuation of Hansen's bibliography, the present work follows fairly closely in his footsteps. Details on the arrangement are given in the notes following the section headings. The basic principles (and the major differences from Hansen) are stated below.

The bibliography restricts itself to Classical Antiquity, from which follows the exclusion of Theology (comprising works by or on Christian writers in antiquity, as well as the Scriptures), Middle Latin, Byzantine Greek (scholia on classical writers excepted), the Classical tradition, and the ancient cultures outside the Classical world. Those are flourishing subjects in Danish scholarship; their inclusion here would in all fairness necessitate going over the years covered by my predecessors once again, to give the full and just picture. Occasional items from those or other neighbouring fields do in fact occur, when found to include material directly relevant to the Classical student; they have been noted as partially (or marginally) relevant, seen from the classicist's point of view.

Titles listed in *Danmark og antikken* are not repeated here, except for doctoral theses of the period 1980-1991, which were included in my bibliography of 1994 as well (due to their extensive summaries in Danish). Translations and reprints of works listed in earlier bibliographies have separate, cross-referenced, entries in the present volume.

The entry format is kept deliberately short, giving author(s); title; parent publication (for articles) or place of publication (for monographs); year of publication; locator (for articles) or pagination (for monographs). Titles are given as found in the original publication, with no attempt to systematize the use of capitals and italics. A content note may be added, together with a parenthetical indication of the item's relevance in this bibliographic context. Illustrations are not noted.

Reviews are treated as articles, titled "Review of ", followed by author, title, place of publication and year of the work reviewed.

The first names of authors and editors are rendered as initials in the entries; the full names of Danish scholars (and the names of Danish co-authors listed as *et al.*) are given in the index of authors. The place of publication is in the modern, national form; København being abbreviated to Kbh. throughout. In entries on multi-volume works, commas separate the publication years, and the page indications, of the individual volumes.

For journal titles of more than one word (and a few other works), standard abbreviations are employed; the full titles are noted in the list of abbreviations. Other parent volumes are given so extensively as to be located in any type of library catalogue.

The content notes are basically meant to supplement the information given in the titles, but a few other pieces of information may be found there as well.

In the entries, [ ] enclose added bibliographical information (most often, the year of publication when differing from the year indicated on the title page). < > mark cross-references within the bibliography, as well as references to the preceding bibliographies of Hansen, the Kristensens, and myself. Omissions in cross-references and in titles of reviewed works are marked by ... , while = indicates, *either* a bilingual title, *or* that the volume in question appeared in a monograph series, *or* that the book is also listed in my bibliography of 1994. Transition from bibliographic information to content notes is indicated by a dash.

The systematic scheme employed by Hansen (based, in its turn, on *L'Année Philologique*), has been mostly retained, although I have added one group and a few subgroups, in order to accomodate expanding subjects within the field, and have suppressed a couple of groups where nothing has been produced during the period.

Generally, I follow Hansen's principles of classification (such as e.g. entering the history and archaeology of a specific locality under Topography). However, during the short time-span covered here (21 years against the 399 years of Hansen's bibliography), works on most classical authors have been relatively sparse. In consequence, sections on individual authors are subdivided by works only, where the number of entries might otherwise confuse the reader, and subdivision by passages eliminated (the information, when not evident from the title, is given in the content notes instead).

Within each section or subsection, the items are listed in chronological order. Reviews are placed under the year when the review appeared, multi-volume works under the year of the first volume. If the year indicated on the title page differs from the actual year of appearance, the latter is used for the chronological arrangement.

For relevant entries listed in other sections, cross-references are provided.

Apart from scholars born, living and working in Denmark I include works by: 1) Danish-born scholars residing abroad, *if* they have published in Denmark (irrespective of language) during the 21 years covered here – thus, I include e.g. the works of Peter Allan Hansen, but not the late works of Harald Ingholt; and 2) Foreign scholars who for a substantial time have worked in Denmark, though only works published during their stay in Denmark – I include e.g. works by Jerker Blomqvist published during his tenure as professor at the University of Copenhagen 1980-1987, but not his earlier and later works.

On both counts, my criteria for inclusion are more restrictive than the principles employed by Hansen, and it is only fair to record that he disagrees with my choice.

A database conversion at a late stage in the work deleted all indications of italics; not all of those may have been restored. For such ancient or modern diacritics as have defied computer typesetting I beg the reader's indulgence. Otherwise, titles are given as found, with no attempt to regulate varying editorial and personal practice as regards the use of capitals in English titles.

Most of the authors have checked their own entries; such mistakes and omissions as still exist are entirely my own.

AUTHORS AND TEXTS

Note. The normal arrangement within each author is chronological. In those few cases where more than ten items have appeared, the items are subdivided as follows: items on several works, or on the author in general; single works (alphabetically arranged); fragments. Text editions are inserted in the chronological sequences, as are items on single passages; as for the latter, the passage in question is indicated in a note, if not evident from the item's title.

Collective headings (Carmina Epigraphica, Itineraria) are found in their alphabetical place among the authors. Titles wrongly but traditionally included in an author's work are to be found there (e.g., Octavia under Seneca, not under the title).

Items on works by two authors are placed under one with a reference from the other.

AESCHYLUS

Generalia et collectanea

Smith, O.L.: Arsenois and *Parisinus Graecus* 2070. In: GRBS 12, 1971, 101-111. – Examines the Oresteia part of the ms. [1

Smith, O.L.: A Note on San Marco 222 and Laur. 31,15. In: C&M 29, 1968 [1972], 16-21. – Dates the scholia ms M to the early 14th cent. [2

Smith, O.L.: Textual Notes on the Scholia to Aeschylus, Oresteia. In: C&M 30, 1969 [1974], 44-55. [3

Jorsal, F.: Vaticanus Graecus 2222 and its Relation to Laur 32,9. In: C&M 31, 1970 [1975], 339-388. – Includes text edition of the scholia in Vat.Gr. 2222. [4

Smith, O.L.: Notes and Observations on some Manuscripts of the Scholia on Aeschylus. In: C&M 31, 1970 [1975], 14-48. [5

Smith, O.L.: Studies in the scholia on Aeschylus. Vol. 1: The recensions of Demetrius Triclinius (= Mnemosyne Supplementum 37). Leiden, 1975. xiv + 288 pp. [6

Friis Johansen, H.: Review of Aeschyli septem quae supersunt tragoedias ed. D. Page. Oxford 1972. In: Gnomon 48, 1976, 321-336. [7

Smith, O.L.: Scholia Graeca in Aeschylum quae exstant omnia. Pars 1 : Scholia in Agamemnonem, Choephoros, Eumenides, Supplices continens. Pars 2:2 : Scholia in Septem adversus Thebas continens. Leipzig, 1976, 1982. xxviii + 218, xxix + 423 pp. [8

Smith, O.L.: Classification of MSS of the Scholia on Aeschylus. In: ICS 6, 1981, 44-55. [9

Smith, O.L.: The So-Called "Sch.Rec." in Editions of the Scholia on Aeschylus. In: Philologus 126, 1982, 138-140. – On Victorinus' versions of the M scholia. [10

Smith, O.L.: Flogging Dead Horses : the Thoman Recension of Aeschylus. In: C&M 37, 1986, 245-254. – On M.H.Shotwell in BZ 77, 1984, 238-256. [11

Agamemnon
Smith, O.L.: *Once Again*: The Guilt of Agamemnon. In: Eranos 71, 1973, 1-11. [12

Choephoroi
Hansen, P.A.: The Robe Episode of the *Choephori*. In: CQ 28, 1978, 239-240. [13

Mejer, J.: Recognizing what, why and when – The Recognition Scene in Aeschylus' Choephori. In: Arktouros, Hellenic Studies Presented to B.M.W. Knox. Berlin, 1979, 115-121. [14

Eumenides
Smith, O.L.: The Scholia on the Eumenids in the Early Triclinian Recension of Aeschylus. In: Philologus 123, 1979, 328-336. [15

Friis Johansen, H.: Aeschylus *Eu*. 566-75. A Diagnosis. In: C&M 39, 1988, 5-14. [16

Prometheus
Smith, O.L.: A new source of Triclinius' commentary on Aeschylus, Prometheus vinctus. In: RhM 117, 1974, 176-180. [17

Smith, O.L.: The commentary in the manuscript *P* of Aeschylus. In: C&M 32, 1971/80 [1980], 11-34. – On the scholia to Prometheus in *Par.gr.* 2781. [18

Septem
Smith, O.L.: The Father's Curse – Some Thoughts on the *Seven against Thebes*. In: C&M 30, 1969 [1974], 27-43. [19

Smith, O.L.: Review of Scholia in Aeschyli Septem adversus Thebas, ed. G. Morocho Gayo. Leon 1989. In: Gnomon 63, 1991, 193-196. [20

Supplices
Friis Johansen, H. & Whittle, E.W.: Textual notes on Aeschylus, Supplices 1-503. In: SymbOsl 50, 1975, 5-41. [21

Aeschylus: The Suppliants. Ed. by H. Friis Johansen and Edward W. Whittle. Vol. 1-3. Kbh., 1980. 120, 517, 480 pp. – Text and commentary. [22

Fragmenta
Smith, O.L.: On Aeschylus, Fragment 638 Mette. In: Glotta 52, 1974, 60-61. – The fragment is ascribed to the scholiast. [23

ALCAEUS

Friis Johansen, H.: Alcaeus and the Kottabos Game. In: Studies in honour of T.B.L. Webster. Bristol, 1986, 93-101. – On Alcaeus 72. [24

ANTHOLOGIA PALATINA

Hansen, P.A.: Review of Citti, V. *et al.*: An Index to the Anthologia Graeca ... Fasc. 1-4 ... Amsterdam 1985-1990. In: CR 37, 1987, 154-155; CR 39, 1989, 386; CR 40, 1990, 472; CR 41, 1991, 472. [25

See also no 1154

ANTHOLOGIA PLANUDEA

Hansen, P.A.: Review of Aubreton, R. & Buffière, F. (eds.): Anthologie grecque. Deuxième partie: Anthologie de Planude, XIII. Paris 1980. In: CR 36, 1986, 205-207. [26

ANTIPHON

Due, B.: Antiphon. A Study in Argumentation (= Opuscula Graecolatina 17). Kbh., 1980. 76 pp. [27

APOLLONIUS TYANAEUS

Hansen, O.: A note on the epigram on Apollonius of Tyana. In: Eranos 81, 1983, 143. [28

APULEIUS

Skafte Jensen, M.: Review of Scobie, A.: Apuleius and Folklore ... London 1983. In: ARV 1985 [1987], 135-136. [29

ARCHIMEDES

Archimedes: Archimedis opera omnia cum commentariis Eutocii iterum edidit Iohan Ludvig Heiberg. Corrigenda adiecit E. S. Stamatis. Vol. 1-3. Stuttgart, 1972. xi + 445, xviii + 554, xcviii + 448 pp. (Reprint of the edition Leipzig 1910-1915 <PAH no 59>). [30

Schmidt, O.: A System of Axioms for the Archimedean Theory of Equilibrium and Centre of Gravity. In: Centaurus 19, 1975, 1-35. [31

ARISTOPHANES

Thomsen, O.: Some Notes on the Thesmophoriazusae 947-1000. In: Classica ... <no 1176>, 1973, 27-46. [32

Jorsal, F.; Kill Jørgensen, M.; Smith, O.[L.]: A Byzantine Metrical Commentary on Aristophanes' *Frogs*. In: C&M 31, 1970 [1975], 324-338. – Introduction and text, based on the mss Modena, Est.α.U.9.22 and Paris, Anc.f.gr.2821. [33

Smith, O.L.: On the Problem of a Thoman Recension of Aristophanes. In: GRBS 17, 1976, 75-80. [34

Smith, O.L.: Urbano da Belluno and Copenhagen GKS 1965, 4to. In: Scriptorium 32, 1978, 57-59. (Partly relevant in touching upon the Aristophanes-ms Kbh. GKS 1980, written by Urbano) [35

Smith, O.L.: Review of Eberline, C.N.: Studies in the Manuscript Tradition of the Ranae ... (= Beiträge z. klass. Philologie 119). Meisenheim 1980. In: Gnomon 55, 1983, 673-676. [36

Thomsen, O.: Drei Emendationen zu den Thesmophoriazusen des Aristophanes: 369, 1019, 1051. In: C&M 39, 1988, 15-18. [37

Hansen, O.: A Note on πικτίδας/πυκτίδας of Aristophanes' Ach. 879. In: Philologus 134, 1990, 158-159. [38

ARISTOTELES

Generalia et collectanea
Collin, F.: The Concept of Substance in the *Categories* and the *Physics*. In: DYPhilos 11, 1974, 72-119. [39

Engberg-Pedersen, T.: Aristotle's Theory of Moral Insight. Oxford, 1983. x + 291 pp. [40

Engberg-Pedersen, T.: Practical Inquiry and Practical Philosophy in Aristotle. In: DYPhilos 22, 1985, 57-63. [41

Ebbesen, S.: New Fragments of "Alexander's" Commentaries on *Analytica Posteriora* and *Sophistici Elenchi*. In: CIMAGL 60, 1990, 113-120. (Partly relevant) [42

Analytica Priora
Engberg-Pedersen, T.: More on Aristotelian Epagoge. In: Phronesis 24, 1979, 301-319. – On *An.Prior.* II,23. [43

Ebbesen, S.: Analysing Syllogisms *or* Anonymus Aurelianensis III – the (presumably) Earliest Extant Latin Commentary on the Prior Analytics, and its Greek Model. In: CIMAGL 37, 1981, 1-20. (Partly relevant) [44

Ἀθηναίων πολιτεία
Hansen, M.H.: Asty, Mesogeios and Paralia. In Defence of Arist. *Ath. Pol.* 21.4. In: C&M 41, 1990, 51-54. [45

See also no 506

Categoriae
Ebbesen, S.: Review of Evangeliou, C.: Aristotele's Categories and Porphyry ... Leiden 1988. In: Isis 82, 1991, 363-364. [46

Ethica Nicomachea
Engberg-Pedersen, T.: Converging Aristotelian Faculties: A Note on *Eth.Nic.* VI.xi.2-3, 1143a25-35. In: JHS 99, 1979, 158-160. [47

Engberg-Pedersen, T.: For Goodness' Sake: More on Nicomachean Ethics I.vii.5. In: AGPh 62,3, 1980, 17-40. [48

Oeconomica
Isager, S.: Once Upon a Time. On the Interpretation of [Aristotle], *Oikonomia* II. In: Studies ... <no 1181>, 1988, 77-83. [49

Rhetorica

Christensen, J.: The Formal Character of *koinoi topoi* in Aristotle's Rhetoric and Dialectic. Illustrated by the List in *Rhetorica* II.23. In: CIMAGL 57, 1988, 3-10. – P. 10 Afterword by Sten Ebbesen. [50

Sophistici Elenchi

Ebbesen, S.: Commentators and commentaries on Aristotle's Sophistici elenchi : a study of post-Aristotelian ancient and medieval writings on fallacies. Vol. 1-3 (= Corpus Latinum commentariorum in Aristotelem Graecorum de Wulf-Mansion Centre 7, 1-3). Leiden, 1981. 351, 555, 414 pp. – Thesis <= DOAII no 67>. (Partly relevant) [51

Bülow-Jacobsen, A. & Ebbesen, S.: Vaticanus Urbinas Graecus 35. An Edition of the Scholia on Aristotele's Sophistici Elenchi. In: CIMAGL 43, 1982, 45-120. – Text pp. 55-113. [52

AVIANUS

Nøjgaard, M.: Review of Küppers, J.: Die Fabeln Avians ... Bonn 1977. In: Gnomon 58, 1986, 366-368. [53

BOETHIUS

Ebbesen, S.: Boethius as an Aristotelian Scholar. In: Aristoteles, Werk und Wirkung, Vol. II. Ed. E. Wiesner. Berlin, 1987, 286-311. – Repr. with minor changes in: Sorabji, R. (ed): Aristotele Transformed, London 1990, 373-391. [54

Ebbesen, S.: Review of Stump, E.: Boethius's In Ciceronis Topica ... Ithaca, N.Y. 1988. In: JHPh 28, 1990, 607-609. [55

Ebbesen, S.: Review of Magee, J.: Boethius on Signification and Mind. London 1990. In: Vivarium 29, 1991, 150-154. [56

CAESAR

Bendz, G.: Novus et inauditus. In: Eranos 80, 1982, 175. – On *De bell.civ.* II 15,1. [57

Lund, A.A.: Zur Frage nach der Urbevölkerung Britanniens (Caes. *Gall.* 5,12,1-3. Tac. *Agr.* 11). In: Gymnasium 95, 1988, 493-504. [58

Lund, A.A.: Drei Emendationsvorschläge zu Caesars Bellum Gallicum. In: Latomus 48, 1989, 93-96. – On *Bell.Gall.* I 30,2; VII 14,5; VII 55,9. [59

See also no 399

CARMINA EPIGRAPHICA GRAECA

Note. Some items of relevance may be found in the section GREEK EPIGRAPHY.

Generalia et collectanea
Hansen, P.A.: A List of Greek Verse Inscriptions down to 400 B. C. : An analytical survey (= Opuscula Graecolatina 3). Kbh., 1975. 53 pp. [60

Hansen, P.A.: Review of Lorenz, B.: Thessalische Grabgedichte ... Innsbruck 1976. In: CR 28, 1978, 381-382. [61

Hansen, P.A.: Review of Häusle, H.: Einfache und frühe Formen des griechischen Epigramms. Innsbruck 1979. In: CR 32, 1982, 34-35. [62

Hansen, P.A.: Review of Pircher, J.: Das Lob der Frau ... Innsbruck 1979. In: CR 32, 1982, 35-36. [63

Hansen, P.A.: Carmina epigraphica Graeca saeculorum VIII-V a.Chr.n (= Texte und Kommentare 12). Berlin, 1983. xxiii + 302 pp. – Addenda and corrigenda in CEG 2 <no 70>, 299-305, and in LGVI 2 <no 68>, 11-13. [64

Hansen, P.A.: Review of Peek, W.: Attische Versinschriften. Berlin 1980. In: CR 33, 1983, 370-371. [65

Hansen, P.A.: Review of Stecher, A.: Inschriftliche Grabgedichte ... Innsbruck 1981. In: CR 33, 1983, 369. [66

Hansen, P.A.: Review of Gallavotti, C.: Metri e ritmi nelle iscrizioni greche. Roma 1979. In: CR 34, 1984, 286-289. [67

Hansen, P.A.: A List of Greek Verse Inscriptions c. 400-300 B.C. With addenda and corrigenda to CEG (LGVI 2) (= Opuscula Graecolatina 28). Kbh., 1985. 52 pp. – Addenda et corrigenda to CEG <no 64> p. 11-13. The corrigendum on CEG no 454 was seperately published as well, as The Date of "Nestor's Cup" in ZPE 58, 1985, 234. [68

Hansen, P.A.: Review of Lausberg, M.: Das Einzeldistichon ... München 1982. In: CR 36, 1986, 207-210. [69

Hansen, P.A.: Carmina Epigraphica Graeca saeculi IV a. Chr. n. (CEG 2) (= Texte und Kommentare 15). Berolini, 1989. 358 pp. – Addenda et corrigenda to CEG 1 <no 64> p. 299-305. [70

Hansen, P.A.: Review of Häusle, H.: Sag mir, o Hund ... Hildesheim 1989. In: CR 40, 1990, 302-303. [71

Specialia
Hansen, P.A.: An Olympic victor by the name of "-kles". An archaic Attic funerary inscription. In: Kadmos 13, 1974, 156-163. [72

Hansen, P.A.: An Epigraphical Ghost-Name. In: ZPE 21, 1976, 37-38. – On SEG XVI 727. [73

Hansen, P.A.: Pithecusan humour. The Interpretation of 'Nestor's Cup' Reconsidered. In: Glotta 54, 1976, 25-43. [74

Hansen, P.A.: DAA 374-375 and the Early Elegiac Epigram. In: Glotta 56, 1978, 195-201. [75

Hansen, O.: On the archaic cenotaph of a proxenos from Kastrades on Corcyra. In: Hermes 115, 1987, 499. – On IG IX,1,867. [76

Hansen, O.: The memorial of Kallimachus reconsidered. In: Hermes 116, 1988, 482-483. [77

Hansen, O.: Nestor's cup. A new suggestion for restoration of the lacune in line 1. In: AC 58, 1988, 280-281. [78

Hansen, O.: The Dipylon Oinochoe once again. In: LCM 15, 1990, 149. – Suggests an alternative reading. Repr. with slightly enlarged illustration in LCM 16, 1991, 3-4. [79

Hansen, P.A.: Diogenes the Cynic at Venice. In: ZPE 82, 1990, 198-200. – The Diogenes epitaph (*Ant.Pal.* vii, 64) in a 17th cent. drawing. [80

CARMINA EPIGRAPHICA LATINA

Krarup, P.: The Faustinus-inscription from Sperlonga. In: Acts V Intern. Congr. of Greek & Latin epigraphy, Cambridge 1969. Oxford, 1971, 215-218. [81

CATULLUS

Bendz, G.: Verborum paria Catulliana. In: Classica ... <no 1176>, 1973, 264-269. – On 14,8; 46,11; 47,5-6. [82

Lund, A.A.: Zum Verständnis des Sappho-Gedichtes (C.51). In: Maia 33, 1981, 147-149. [83

Ingemann, V.: *Albus an Ater* : A Double Entendre in Catullus 93? In: C&M 33, 1981/82, 146-150. [84

Lund, A.A.: Zur korrekten Restitution des zweiten Gedichtes Catulls. In: Maia 38, 1986, 153-158. [85

Laursen, S.: The Apple of Catullus 65 : A Love Pledge of Callimachus. In: C&M 40, 1989, 161-169. [86

CICERO

Krarup, P.: Scipio Aemilianus as a Defender of Kingship. A Contribution to the Interpretation of Cicero's De re publica. In: Classica ... <no 1176>, 1973, 209-223. [87

Krarup, P.: Quelques remarques sur l'originalité de Cicéron dans ses oeuvres politiques. In: Mélanges de philosophie, de littérature et d'histoire ancienne offerts à P. Boyancé (= CEFR 22). Rome, 1974, 455-460. [88

Munk Olsen, B.: Quelques aspects de la diffusion du Somnium Scipionis de Cicéron au Moyen Age. In: Studia Romana ... <no 1177>, 1976, 146-153. [89

COLUMELLA

Lund, A.A.: Nochmals Columella 6,1,1. In: Eranos 80, 1982, 174. [90

CORINNA

Hansen, O.: The meaning of Corinna's ϝεροια reconsidered. In: HSF 102, 1989, 70-71. [91

CORPUS HERMETICUM

Giversen, S.: Hermetic Communities? In: Rethinking Religion <no 1097>, 1989, 49-54. [92

CURTIUS RUFUS

Lund, A.A.: Neues zur Curtius 3,5,1. 3,10,5. 4,10,3. In: Gymnasium 94, 1987, 438-441. [93

See also no 227

DEMETRIUS MAGNESIUS

Mejer, J.: Demetrius of Magnesia: On Poets and Authors of the Same Name. In: Hermes 109, 1981, 447-472. – Text edition of Περὶ ὁμονύμων ποιητῶν καὶ συγγραφέων. [94

DEMOSTHENES

Due, B.: Kritisches zu der Proklesis in [Dem.] LIX. In: Classica ... <no 1176>, 1973, 85-91. – On *Against Neaira* 124. [95

Hansen, M.H.: Two Notes on Demosthenes' Symbouleutic Speeches. In: C&M 35, 1984, 57-70. – Contents: I. Were Demosthenes' Symbouleutic Speeches Delivered in Support of Proposals?; II. Demosthenes' Publication of his Symbouleutic Speeches. Repr. with addenda in: The Athenian Ecclesia 2 <no 530>, 283-297. [96

DIOGENES LAERTIUS

Mejer, J.: Diogenes Laertius and his Hellenistic background (= Hermes Einzelschriften 40). Wiesbaden, 1978. 108 pp. – Thesis. [97

EPICURUS

Laursen, S.: Epicurus, On Nature Book XXV. In: CronErcol 17, 1987, 77-78. [98

Laursen, S.: Epicurus "On Nature" XXV (Long-Sedley 20 B, C and j). In: CronErcol 18, 1988, 7-18. [99

Laursen, S.: "Against Democritus – towards the end". In: Miscellanea papyrologica in occassione del bicentenario dell'edizione della Charta Borgiana, Vol. I. Eds. M. di Capasso *et al.* (= Papyrologica Florentina 19). Firenze, 1990, 3-22. – Reconstruction of Epicurus fr. 34 Arrigh. through P.Herc. 697, 1056, 1191. [100

EUCLIDES

Euclides: Evclidis elementa. Post I.L.Heiberg ed. E.S.Stamatis. Vol. 1-5.2. Leipzig, 1969, 1970, 1972, 1973, 1977, 1977. xlii + 190, viii + 239, xxxii + 236, xxxi + 238, lxxxix + 243, v + 362 pp. (Partial reprint (omitting the translation) of the edition Leipzig 1883-1916 <PAH no 368>). [101

Taisbak, C.M.: Division and Logos. A Theory of Equivalent Couples and Sets of Integers Propounded by Euclid in the Arithmetical Books of the Elements (= Acta Historica Scientiarum Naturalium et Medicinalium 25). Odense, 1971. 128 pp. – Thesis. [102

Taisbak, C.M.: Perfect numbers. A mathematical pun? In: Centaurus 20, 1976, 269-275. – On Euclid *Elementa* IX. [103

Taisbak, C.M.: Coloured Quadrangles. A Guide to the Tenth Book of Euclid's Elements (= Opuscula Graecolatina 24). Kbh., 1982. 78 pp. [104

Taisbak, C.M.: Elements of Euclid's *Data*. In: ΠΕΡΙ ΤΩΝ ΜΑΘΗΜΑΤΩΝ = Peri Ton Mathematon. Ed. I. Mueller (= Apeiron 1990,4). Edmonton, 1990, 135-171. [105

EURIPIDES

Smith, O.L.: Scholia metrica anonyma in Euripidis, Hecubam, Orestem, Phoenissas (= Opuscula Graecolatina 10). Kbh., 1977. xxv + 69 pp. [106

Schartau, B.: Observations of the commentary of Euripides Phoenissae in the mss. Parm. 154 and Modena α.U.9.22. In: ICS 6, 1981, 221-241. [107

Blomqvist, J.: Human and divine action in Euripides' Hippolytus. In: Hermes CX, 1982, 398-414. [108

Smith, O.L.: On the Scribal Hands in the MS P of Euripides. In: Mnemosyne 35, 1982, 326-331. – Identification of two scribal hands in Vat.Pal.gr. 287 + Laur. C.S. 172. [109

See also no 363

FRONTINUS

Frontinus: Strategemata = Kriegslisten. Lateinisch und deutsch von G. Bendz. Berlin, 1978. 262 pp. (Reprint of the edition Berlin 1963 <PAH no 400>). [110

GALENUS

Ebbesen, S.: Galeni libellus de captionibus. New Manuscripts. In: Hermes 101, 1973, 374-379. [111

HERO

Drachmann, A.G.: Heron's Model of the Universe (Pneumatics 2:7). In: Actes XII Congr. Intern. d'Histoire des Sciences, Paris 1968. Paris, 1971, 47-50. [112

Smith, O.L.: On some manuscripts of Heron, Pneumatica. In: Scriptorium 27, 1973, 96-101. [113

Taisbak, C.M.: An Archimedean Proof of Heron's Formula for the Area of a Triangle. Reconstructed. In: Centaurus 24, 1980, 110-116. – Errata in Centaurus 25, 1981/82, p. 160. [114

Heron: Les méchaniques ou l'élévateur des corps lourds, texte arabe de Qusta Ibn Luqa établi et trad. par B. Carra de Vaux, introd. de D.R. Hill, comm. par A.G. Drachmann. Paris, 1988. 420 pp. – Text and translation are reprinted from the edition Paris 1894, the commentary consists of extracts from Drachmann's The Mechanical Technology of Greek and Roman Antiquity, Kbh., 1963 <PAH no 3151>. [115

HESIODUS

Breitenstein, T.: Hésiode et Archiloque (= Odense University Classical Studies 1). Odense, 1971. 70 pp. [116

Andersen, L.: The *Shield of Heracles*. Problems of Genesis. In: C&M 30, 1969 [1974], 10-26. [117

Smith, O.L.: Review of Scholia vetera in Hesiodi Theogoniam, ed. L. di Gregorio. Milano 1975. In: BZ 72, 1979, 39-40. [118

Skafte Jensen, M.: Review of Hamilton, R.: The Architecture of Hesiodic Poetry, Baltimore 1989, and of Schhmidt, J.U.: Adressat und Paraineseform ... Göttingen 1986. In: CR 40, 1990, 213-214. [119

Skafte Jensen, M.: Review of Sihvola, J.: Decay, Progress, the Good Life? Hesiod and Protagoras ... Helsinki 1989. In: CR 41, 1991, 89-90. [120

HOMERICI HYMNI

Lundager Jensen, H.J.: Von Delos zu Babel. In: LingBibl H. 59, 1987, 65-75. (Partly relevant, touching upon the Apollo hymn) [121

HOMERUS

Skafte Jensen, M.: The Homeric question and the oral-formulaic theory (= Opuscula Graecolatina 20). Kbh., 1980. 226 pp. – Thesis <=DOAII no 176>. [122

Skafte Jensen, M.: A Note on Homer's Use of the Word κραναός. In: C&M 33, 1981/82, 5-8. [123

Pade, M.: Homer's Catalogue of Women. In: C&M 34, 1983, 7-15. – On *Od.* XI 225-332. [124

Skafte Jensen, M.: Storia e verità nei poemi omerici. In: QUCC 22, 1986, 21-35. [125

Skafte Jensen, M.: Homeeriset eepokset ja kreikalainen kulttuuri-identiteetii. In: Kalevala ja maailman eepokset. Ed. L. Honko. Helsinki, 1987, 23-36. [126

Skafte Jensen, M.: The variability of Homeric poetry. In: Acta II journées d'études en littérature orale, Paris 23.-26.3.1987. Ed. V. Görög-Karady. Paris, 1989, 281-287. [127

Skafte Jensen, M.: Homer. In: Enzyklopädie des Märchens, Vol. 6. Ed. K. Ranke *et al.* Berlin, 1990, 1205-1218. [128

Skafte Jensen, M.: The Homeric epics and Greek cultural identity. In: Religion, Myth, and Folklore in the World's Epics. The Kalevala and its Predecessors. Ed. L. Honko. Berlin & New York, 1990, 29-48. [129

HORATIUS

Smith, O.L.: A reading of Horace, Carm. I,15. In: C&M 29, 1968 [1972], 67-74. [130

Smith, H.: Nunc est Bibendum – A Literary Analysis of Horace's Cleopatra Ode (I,37). In: Classica ... <no 1176>, 1973, 280-289. [131

Sørensen, S.: Horace *Ars Poetica* 317-318. In: C&M 38, 1987, 113-120. [132

Friis-Jensen, K.: Horatius liricus et ethicus. Two twelfth-century school texts on Horace's poems. In: CIMAGL 57, 1988, 81-147. (Partly relevant) [133

IAMBLICUS

Dalsgaard Larsen, B.: Jamblique de Chalcis, exégète et philosophe. Vol. 1-2. Århus, 1972. 510, 137 pp. – Thesis. [134

Dalsgaard Larsen, B.: La place de Jamblique dans la philosophie antique tardive. In: De Jamblique à Proclus. Ed. H. Doerrie (= Entretiens Hardt 21). Genève, 1975, 1-34. [135

Dalsgaard Larsen, B.: Un temoignage grec tardif sur Jamblique et la tradition platonicienne: Athanase le Rheteur. In: CIMAGL 20, 1977, 1-37. (Partly relevant) [136

IOSEPHUS

Mejer, J. & Raasted, J.: A Note on Josephus Latinus in Denmark. In: Classica ... <no 1176>, 1973, 371-382. [137

Bilde, P.: The Causes of the Jewish War According to Josephus. In: JSJ 10, 1979, 179-202. [138

Bilde, P.: Studier i Josefus og kristendommens grundlæggelse. Stavtrup, 1982. 75 pp. – Summary in English p. 1-8. The volume contains a reprint of Causes ... <no 138>, as well as of several articles in Danish. – Thesis <= DOAII no 198>. [139

Bilde, P.: Major Trends in Modern Josephus Research. In: NordJud 8, 1987, 73-105. [140

Bilde, P.: Flavius Josephus Between Jerusalem and Rome. His Life, his Works, and their Importance (= JSP Supplement series 2). Sheffield, 1988. 272 pp. [141

ISAEUS

Isager, S.: The Marriage Pattern in Classical Athens : Men and Women in Isaios. In: C&M 33, 1981/82, 81-96. [142

ISOCRATES

Due, O.S.: The Date of Isocrates' *Areopagiticus*. In: Studies ... <no 1181>, 1988, 84-90. [143

ITINERARIA

Blomqvist, J.: Reflections of Carthagenian Commercial Activity in Hanno's Periplus. In: On the Dignity of Man. Oriental and Classical Studies in Honour of Frithiof Rundgren. Stockholm, 1986, 53-62. [144

IUVENALIS

Fruelund Jensen, B.: Crime, vice and retribution in Juvenal's Satires. In: C&M 33, 1981/82, 155-168. [145

Fruelund Jensen, B.: Martyred and Beleaguered Virtue : Juvenal's Portrait of Umbricius. In: C&M 37, 1986, 185-197. – On Sat. III. [146

LACTANTIUS

Søby Christensen, A.: Lactantius the Historian : An Analysis of the *De Mortibus Persecutorum* (= Opuscula Graecolatina 21). Kbh., 1980. 119 pp. [147

MATERNUS

Kragelund, P.: Vatinius, Nero and Curiatius Maternus. In: CQ 37, 1987, 197-202. [148

MELA

Lund, A.A.: Zu Pomponius Mela 3,20 und 3,54. In: C&M 42, 1991, 241-246. – New readings proposed. [149

MELANIPPIDES

Hansen, O.: Melanippides fr 762 PMG written by Euripides? In: ŽivaAnt 36, 1986, 32. [150

MENANDER

Bülow-Jacobsen, A.: A Fragment of Dialogue in Iambics. ? Menander ? φάνιον. In: BICS 24, 1977, 64-66. [151

Blomqvist, J.: Τὴν θύραν πέπληχεν. In: C&M 38, 1987, 81-90. – On the sense of the verb, occurring five times in Menander. [152

OVIDIUS

Due, O.S.: Kritisches zu Ovids Fasten II, 115. In: C&M 29, 1968 [1972], 61-66. [153

Due, O.S.: Changing forms : Studies in the Metamorphoses of Ovid (= C&M Dissertationes 10). Kbh., 1974. 210 pp. – Thesis. [154

Due, O.S.: Amores und Abtreibung: Ov. *Am.* II 13 & 14. In: C&M 32, 1971/80 [1980], 133-150. [155

Due, O.S.: Ovid's Amores and Abortion. In: Mosaic 12/2, 1981, 37-53. – Revised English version of Amores ... <no 155>. [156

Friis Johansen, H.: Ovid Met. 9.777-8 : the Sound of What and the What of the Rattles? In: C&M 40, 1989, 183-189. [157

PAUSANIAS

Jeppesen, K.: Ἀργοῦσά που κατὰ τὸ θεῖον: Zu Pausanias IX 4,2 über die Gemälde im Tempel der Athena Areia zu Plataä. In: AArch 42, 1971 [1972], 110-112. [158

See also no 316

PETRONIUS

Lund, A.A.: Zu Petronius C 40,1. In: C&M 39, 1988, 207-208. [159

Kragelund, P.: Epicurus, Priapus and the Dreams in Petronius. In: CQ 39, 1989, 436-450. [160

PHILO IUDAEUS

Giversen, S.: L'expérience mystique chez Philon. In: Mysticism. Eds. S.S. Hartman & C.M. Edsman (= Scripta Instituti Donneriani Aboensis V). Stockholm, 1970, 91-98. [161

PHILODEMUS

Boserup, I.: Zu Philodems De Pietate und Heraklit B80. In: ZPE 8, 1971, 109-115. [162

PINDARUS

Friis Johansen, H.: Agesias, Hieron and Pindar's Sixth Olympian Ode. In: Classica ... <no 1176>, 1973, 1-9. [163

Ebbesen, S.: Pindaros O. I,106-108. In: Hermes 102, 1974, 503. [164

Smith, O.L.: Pindar's Seventh Nemean Ode. In: C&M 35, 1984, 5-17. [165

Fisker, D.: Pindars erste Olympische Ode (= Odense University Classical Studies 15). Odense, 1990. 96 pp. [166

PLATO

Ostenfeld, E.[N.]: Disorderly Motion in the *Timaeus*. In: C&M 29, 1968 [1972], 22-26. [167

Ostenfeld, E.[N.]: Plato's Concept of Matter. In: Classica ... <no 1176>, 1973, 47-67. [168

Mejer, J.: Review of Platon, Phèdre. Traduction ... par P. Vicaire. Paris 1972. In: CW 68, 1974, 212-213. [169

Mejer, J.: Review of Weingartner, R.H.: The Unity of the Platonic Dialogue ... New York 1973. In: CP 71, 1975, 365-367. [170

Ostenfeld, E.N.: Forms, matter and mind : three strands in Plato's metaphysics (= Martinus Nijhoff philosophy library 10). The Hague, 1982. xi + 347 pp. [171

Ostenfeld, E.[N.]: Plato's Development and the Date of the *Timaeus*. In: C&M 37, 1986, 63-87. [172

Ostenfeld, E.N.: Self-Motion, Tripartition and Embodiment. In: C&M 41, 1990, 43-49. – On Plato's theory of knowledge. [173

Ostenfeld, E.[N.]: The foundation of Socratic morality. In: Méthexis 4, 1991, 5-18. [174

PLAUTUS

Ussing, J.L.: Commentarius in Plauti comoedias. Denuo edendum curavit indicibus auxit A. Thierfelder (Teildruck). Vol. 1-2. Hildesheim, New York, 1972. 821, 612 pp. (Partial reprint (omitting the text) of the edition Kbh. 1875-1886 <PAH no 850>). [175

Torresin, G.: Sull'Aulularia di Plauto. In: Classica ... <no 1176>, 1973, 167-193. [176

PLINIUS MAIOR

Isager, J.: The Composition of Pliny's Chapters on the History of Art. In: ARID 6, 1971, 49-62. [177

Bülow-Jacobsen, A.: Principatus Medio. Pliny N.H. XIII, 72 sqq.. In: ZPE 20, 1976, 113-116. – Pliny on papyrus production. [178

Bülow-Jacobsen, A.: 'Magna in latitudine earum differentia' (Pliny, NH XIII,78). In: ZPE 60, 1985, 273-274. – Pliny on papyrus production. [179

Isager, J.: Plinio il Vecchio e le meraviglie di Roma : *Mirabilia in terris* e *Romae miracula* nel XXXVI libro della *Naturalis Historia*. In: ARID 15, 1986, 37-50. [180

Pedersen, O.: Some astronomical topics in Pliny. In: Pliny the Elder, his sources and influence. Ed. R. French & F. Greenaway. London, 1986, 162-196. [181

Isager, J.: Pliny on Art and Society : The Elder Pliny's Chapters on the History of Art. London, 1991. 255 pp. – Thesis <= DOAII no 271>. [182

PLINIUS MINOR

Bek, L.: Ut ars natura – ut natura ars : Le ville di Plinio e il concetto del giardino nel Rinascimento. In: ARID 7, 1974, 109-156. (The section pp. 112-120: Le ville pliniane, is of relevance) [183

PLOTINUS

Friis Johansen, K.: Plotinus on human freedom. In: Greek and Latin studies in memory of Caius Fabricius. Ed. S.-T. Teodorsson. Göteborg, 1990, 220-238. [184

PLUTARCHUS

Hansen, P.A.: Pletho and Herodotean malice. In: CIMAGL 12, 1974, 1-10. – On Pletho's excerpts from De herodoti malignitate in Marc. Gr. 517. [185

Plutarchus: Πλουτάρχου περὶ τῆς ‘Ηροδότου κακοηθείας = Plutarchi de Herodoti malignitate, edidit P.A. Hansen. Amsterdam, 1979. xviii + 77 pp. [186

POLYBIUS

Mørkholm, O.: The Speech of Agelaus Again. In: Chiron 4, 1974, 127-132. – On 5. 105.4-9 <cf. PAH no 884>. [187

PORPHYRIUS

Ebbesen, S.: Porphyry's legacy to logic: a reconstruction. In: Aristotele Transformed. The Ancient Commentators and Their Influence. Ed. R. Sorabji. London, 1990, 141-171. [188

POSIDONIUS

Taisbak, C.M.: Posidonius Vindicated at all Costs? Modern Scholarship versus the Stoic Earth Measurer. In: Centaurus 18, 1974, 253-269. – Points out that Posidonius' ideas are misrepresented by Ptolemaios. [189

See also no 264

PROPERTIUS

Due, O.S.: Two notes on Propertius 1,16,44 and 4,8,5 ff. In: C&M 33, 1981/82, 151-154. [190

Due, O.S.: La première Elégié de Properce. In: C&M 36, 1985, 159-171. [191

Friis-Jensen, K.: Propertius 1,18,19 : A Conjecture. In: C&M 36, 1985, 173-175. [192

PTOLEMAEUS

Pedersen, O.: A Survey of the Almagest (= Acta Historica Scientiarum Naturalium et Medicinalium 30). Odense, 1974. 454 pp. [193

Taisbak, C.M.: Eleven Eighty-Thirds. Ptolemy's reference to Eratosthenes in Almagest I.12. In: Centaurus 27, 1984, 165-166. [194

Moesgaard, K.P.: Review of Newton, Robert R.: The Origins of Ptolemy's Astronomical Parameters; College Park, Md. 1982. In: Centaurus 28, 1985, 69-71. [195

Andersen, K.: The Central Projection in One of Ptolemy's Map Constructions. In: Centaurus 30, 1987, 106-113. – On VII,6. [196

Moesgaard, K.P.: In Chase of an Origin for the Mean Planetary Motions in Ptolemy's *Almagest*. In: From Ancient Omens to Statistical Mechanics. Essays on the Exact Sciences Presented to Asger Aaboe. Copenhagen, 1987, 43-54. (Partly relevant, postulating origin in the Babylonian praxis of parallel countings of synodic phenomena for the planets and for the moon) [197

QUINTILIANUS

Kragelund, P.: Epicurus, Pseudo-Quintilian and the Rhetor at Trajan's Forum. In: C&M 42, 1991, 259-275. – On [Quintillianus] *Declamatio major* X. [198

SALLUSTIUS

Smith, H.: Factio, Factiones and the Nobilitas in Sallust. In: C&M 29, 1968 [1972], 187-196. [199

Smith, O.L.: Zu Sallust, Epistulae ad Caesarem II, 7, 6. In: Classica ... <no 1176>, 1973, 262-263. [200

Christensen, J.: Soli Innocentes : A note on a possible political term in Sallust. In: Studia Romana ... <no 1177>, 1976, 41-43. [201

Due, O.S.: La position politique de Salluste. In: C&M 34, 1983, 113-139. [202

SENECA (RHETOR)

Due, O.S.: Der alte Seneca und Annaeus Mela. In: Studia Romana ... <no 1177>, 1976, 60-63. – On Contr. 2, praefatio. [203

SENECA (PHILOSOPHUS)

Generalia et collectanea
Thomsen, O.: Seneca the story-teller. The structure and function, the humour and psychology of his stories. In: C&M 32, 1971/80 [1980], 151-197. [204

Sørensen, V.: Seneca : ein Humanist an Neros Hof. München, 1984. 320 pp. – Translation of Seneca : humanisten ved Neros hof. Kbh., 1976 <DOAI no 353>. – Repr. Zürich 1986. [205

Sørensen, V.: Seneca : the humanist at the court of Nero. Edinburgh, 1984. 352 pp, 16 pls. – Translation of Seneca ... <cf. no 205>. [206

Sørensen, V.: Seneca. Roma, 1988. 396 pp, 8 pls. – Translation of Seneca ... <cf. no 205>. [207

Lund, A.A.: Weitere Emendationen zu Seneca. In: Hermes 117, 1989, 485-495. – Emendations to *Apoc.*, *Dial.* and *Clem.*. [208

Apocolocyntosis
Bruun, N.W.: Kritische Bemerkungen zur Apocolocyntosis des Seneca. In: ARID 15, 1986, 19-35. [209

Bruun, N.W.: Zur Editio Princeps der Apocolocyntosis und ihren Textverhältnissen. In: C&M 39, 1988, 209-216. [210

Lund, A.A.: Zur Restitution von Sen. *Apoc.* c.11,2. In: Philologus 133, 1989, 158-162. [211

Bruun, N.W.: Neue Bemerkungen zur Apocolocyntosis des Seneca. In: ARID 19, 1990, 69-78. [212

Lund, A.A.: Zur Herstellung von Senecas Apocolocyntosis 6,1 und 10,3. In: WJA 17, 1991, 241-247. [213

Consolatio ad Marciam, see no 353

Dialogi
Lund, A.A.: Drei Emendationsvorschläge zu Seneca (dial. III 20,5; VI 3,4; VI 18,7). In: Maia 39, 1987, 127-129. [214

Epistulae
Bruun, N.W.: Marginalia ad Senecae epistulas. In: Eranos 87, 1989, 74-76. – Publication of Bertil Axelson's marginal notes to Seneca's Letters (in the Oxford edition). [215

Hippolytus
Skovgaard-Hansen, M.: The Fall of Phaeton. Meaning in Seneca's 'Hippolytus'. In: C&M 29, 1968 [1972], 92-123. [216

Octavia
Kragelund, P.: Prophecy, Populism, and Propaganda in the "Octavia" (= Opuscula Graecolatina 25). Kbh., 1982. 88 pp. [217

Kragelund, P.: The Prefect's Dilemma and the Date of the *Octavia*. In: CQ 38, 1988, 492-508. [218

SOPHOCLES

Smith, O.L.: Review of Christodoulou, G.: Τὰ ἀρχαῖα σχόλια εἰς Αἴαντα τοῦ Σοφοκλέους ... Athens 1977. In: CR 29, 1979, 12-14. [219

Smith, O.L.: A note on the Sophocles MS *Vat.Gr.* 1333. In: C&M 32, 1971/80 [1980], 35-43. [220

Friis Johansen, H: Heracles in Sophocles' *Trachiniae*. In: C&M 37, 1986, 47-61. – Paper read at the 8th Cong. of the Intern. federation of the Societies of classical studies; Dublin, august 1984. [221

Friis Johansen, H.: Review of Kamerbeek, C.J.: The plays of Sophocles. Commentaries VII: The Oedipus Coloneus. Leiden 1984. In: Gnomon 59, 1987, 198-202. [222

Skouvig, A.C.: Sophocles, *Electra* 77-85. In: C&M 40, 1989, 135-144. [223

STATIUS

Lund, A.A.: "Richtig" und "echt" als Begriffe der Textkritik (Anmerkungen zu Stat. *silv.* 2,1,83 f., 2,1,157 f. u. 2,5,1 f.). In: Mnemosyne 42, 1989, 116-119. [224

TACITUS

Generalia et collectanea
Lund, A.A.: Zum Germanenbegriff bei Tacitus. In: Germanenprobleme in heutiger Sicht. Ed. H. Beck. 1986, 53-87. [225

Bruun, N.W.: Der Anakoluth bei Tacitus. In: Maia 39, 1987, 137-138. [226

Lund, A.A.: Lexikalische und kritische Bemerkungen zur Tacitus und Curtius Rufus. In: Gymnasium 94, 1987, 50-56. [227

See also no 399

Agricola
Lund, A.A.: De Agricola primo inventore. In: Gymnasium 87, 1980, 281-282. [228

Lund, A.A.: On the use of linguistics in connection with textual criticism illustrated by Tac. *Agr.* 12.2. In: C&M 32, 1971/80 [1980], 199-202. [229

Lund, A.A.: Three conjectures in Tacitus' *Agricola*. In: CQ 32, 1982, 178-180. – On 6,4; 9,3; 44,2. [230

Lund, A.A.: Zu den Rassenkriterien des Tacitus. In: Latomus 41, 1982, 845-849. – On *Agr.* XI,1,3. [231

Lund, A.A.: Physiognomica im *Agricola* des Tacitus (45,1-2). In: Maia 36, 1984, 165-167. [232

Lund, A.A.: De causis corruptae lectionis cuiusdam quam in Taciti Agricola inesse suspicor emendandae. In: RhM 130, 1987, 188-190. – On *Agr.* 3,2. [233

Lund, A.A.: Review of Heubner, H.: Kommentar zum *Agricola* des Tacitus. Göttingen 1984. In: Gnomon 59, 1987, 355-357. – Also review by Lund of same work in Latomus 47, 1988, 161-163. [234

See also no 58

Annales
Lund, A.A.: Zu drei unechten Stellen in den *Ann.* des Tacitus. In: Mnemosyne 42, 1989, 124-128. – On 1 8,3; 1 25,2; 6 6,1. [235

Bruun, N.W.: Zu Tac. *Ann.* 16,2,1. In: Eranos 89, 1991, 123-124. [236

Germania
Bruun, N.W.: Über eine schwierige Tacitusstelle. In: WS Neue Folge 8, 1974, 154-155. – On *Germ.* 38.2. [237

Lund, A.A.: A Note on Tacitus' Germania 36,1. In: C&M 31, 1970 [1975], 130-131. [238

Lund, A.A.: On the Meaning of a much discussed passage in the Germania of Tacitus (26, 1-2). In: C&M 31, 1970 [1975], 124-129. [239

Bruun, N.W.: Annotationes criticae in Taciti Germaniam. In: SymbOsl 51, 1976, 137-144. [240

Lund, A.A.: De Germaniae vocabulo (Taciti *Germaniae* 2,5). In: Glotta 55, 1977, 93-111. [241

Lund, A.A.: Nochmals zur Katastrophe der Cherusker (Tac. Germ. 36,1). In: Gymnasium 85, 1978, 179-181. [242

Lund, A.A.: *Pariendum* oder *pereundum?* (Tac. *Germ.* 18.4). In: SymbOsl 54, 1979, 119-123. [243

Lund, A.A.: Tac. Germ. 46,1-2. In: Gymnasium 86, 1979, 75-80. [244

Bruun, N.W.: Kritische Bemerkungen zur Germania des Tacitus. In: Gymnasium 87, 1980, 431-435. – On 45,2 and 45,5. [245

Bruun, N.W. & Lund, A. A.: Zu den vermeintlichen Glossemen in der Germania des Tacitus. In: Gymnasium 88, 1981, 505-511. [246

Lund, A.A.: Zur Beschreibung der Fennen in der "Germania" des Tacitus. In: ZfdA 110, 1981, 241-243. [247

Lund, A.A.: Neue Studien zum Verständnis der Namensätze in der Germania des Tacitus (2,2 und 2,3). In: Gymnasium 89, 1982, 296-327. [248

Kristensen, A.K.G.: Tacitus' germanische Gefolgschaft (= HistFilosMed 50:5). Kbh., 1983. 93 pp. [249

Lund, A.A.: Neues zu Tac. *Germ.* 46,2. In: SymbOsl 58, 1983, 117-121. [250

Lund, A.A.: Review of Kristensen, A.K.G.: Tacitus' germanische Gefolgschaft. Kbh. 1983. In: Gymnasium 91, 1984, 365-366. – <Cf. no 249> [251

Lund, A.A.: Review of P. Cornelius Tacitus, Germania, ed. A. Önnerfors. Stuttgart 1983. In: Gymnasium 91, 1984, 363-365. [252

Lund, A.A.: Zur Glaubwürdigkeit der Germania des Tacitus. Tac. Germ. 12 und 27. In: Eranos 82, 1984, 205-210. [253

Lund, A.A.: Ist Decumates agri eine Textverderbnis? (Tacitus, Germania, 29,3). In: Latomus 44, 1985, 337-350. [254

Lund, A.A.: Neues zum mantischen Schlachtgesang der Germanen (Tac. Germ. 3,1). In: Maia 37, 1985, 263-270. [255

Lund, A.A.: Review of Kraggerud, E.: Der Namensatz der Taciteischen Germania. Oslo, 1981. In: Latomus 44, 1985, 222-223. – On *Germ.* 2,2-3. [256

Lund, A.A.: Zur "Agrarverfassung" der Germanen (Tac. Germ. Kap. 26). In: SymbOsl 60, 1985, 121-127. [257

Lund, A.A.: Neues zu Tac. Germ. 38. In: RhM 130, 1987, 58-67. [258

Lund, A.A.: Zur Lakune in Tac. Germ. 38,2. In: RhM 130, 1987, 346-349. [259

Lund, A.A.: Wie benutzten die Germanen zu Tacitus' Zeiten die römische Münzen? In: JNG 37-38, 1987-88, 41-15. – Points out that *Germ.* 5 is at variance with the archaeological record, and suggests that the passage is a criticism of Nero's monetary reform. [260

Lund, A.A.: Physiognomica in der 'Germania' des Tacitus. In: RhM 131, 1988, 358-369. [261

Lund, A.A.: Zu Tac. Germ. 30,1. In: RhM 131, 1988, 162-167. [262

Tacitus, P. Cornelius: Germania : interpretiert, herausgegeben, übertragen, kommentiert und mit einer Bibliographie versehen von Allan A. Lund. Heidelberg, 1988. 282 pp, 24 pls. [263

Hansen, O.: Did Poseidonios give Germania her name? In: Latomus 48, 1989, 878-879. – On *Germ.* 2,3. [264

Lund, A.A.: Probleme der Germania-Forschung. In: Philologus 133, 1989, 260-277. [265

Lund, A.A.: Zu den Suebenbegriffen in der taciteischen Germania. In: Klio 71, 1989, 620-635. – On *Germ.* 38. [266

Lund, A.A.: Kritischer Forschungsbericht zur "Germania" des Tacitus. In: ANRW 2,33,3. Berlin, 1991, 1989-2222; 2341-2344. – Indices pp. 2347-2382. [267

Lund, A.A.: Zur Gesamtinterpretation der "Germania" des Tacitus. In: ANRW 2,33,3. Berlin, 1991, 1858-1988. – Includes Anhang: Zu Entstehung und Geschichte des Namens und Begriffs "Germani" pp. 1956-1988. Indices pp. 2347-2382. [268

THEOGNIS

Friis Johansen, H.: A poem by Theognis (Thgn. 19-38). In: C&M 42, 1991, 5-37. [269

THEOPHRASTUS

Engberg-Pedersen, T.: Review of Fortenbaugh, W.W., Huby, P.M. & Long A.A. (eds.): Theophrastus of Eresus ... New Brunswick & Oxford 1985, and of Gaiser, K.: Theophrast in Assos ... Heidelberg 1985. In: CR 37, 1987, 53-57. [270

Hansen, O.: The Ploia-Wood in Theophrastus Historia Plantarum 5,4,7. In: Sprachwissenschaft 12, 1987, 110. [271

See also no 366

THUCYDIDES

Bülow-Jacobsen, A.: A Third-Century Codex of Thucydides. In: BICS 22, 1975, 65-83. – On P.Oxy. ined. 39 5B 117/E (3-4). [272

Mørch, S.: Popularité ou impopularité d'Athènes chez Thucydide. In: C&M 31, 1970 [1975], 49-71. [273

Christensen, J. & Hansen, M.H.: What is *Syllogos* at Thukydides 2.22.1? In: C&M 34, 1983, 17-31. – Repr. with addenda in: The Athenian Ecclesia 2 <no 530>, 195-211. [274

TIMOTHEUS

Hansen, O.: On the date and place of the first performance of Timotheus' Persae. In: Philologus 128, 1984, 135-138. – Proposes performance at the Athenian Munichia 410/9. [275

Hansen, O.: The So-called Prayer to the Fates and Timotheus' *Persae*. In: RhM 133, 1990, 190-193. [276

VERGILIUS

Hansen, P.A.: *Ille ego qui quondam* ... Once Again. In: CQ 22, 1972, 139-149. – Suggests that Vergil may be the author. [277

Due, O.S.: Zur Etymologisierung in der Aeneis. In: Classica ... <no 1176>, 1973, 270-279. [278

Kragelund, P.: Dream and Prediction in the Aeneid : A Semiotic Interpretation of the Dreams of Aeneas and Turnus (= Opuscula Graecolatina 7). Kbh., 1976. 91 pp. [279

Bruun, N.W.: Rossia, eine vox nihili. In: RhM 132, 1989, 410. – On Schol. Verg. Bern. georg 2,86. [280

VITRUVIUS

Jeppesen, K.: Did Vitruvius ever visit Halikarnassos? In: Anadolu 22, 1981-83 [1989], 85-98. [281

Jeppesen, K.: Vitruvius in Africa. In: Munus non ingratum. Proceed. of the intern. symposium on Vitruvius De Architectura and the Hellenistic and Republican architecture, Leiden 20-23 January 1987. Ed. H. Geertman & J.J. De Jong (= BABesch Supplement 2). Leiden, 1989, 31-33. [282

XENOPHON

Xenophon: Expeditio Cyri, ed. C. Hude. Ed. correct. cur. J. Peters. Leipzig, 1972. xx + 330 pp. (Reprint with corrections of the edition Leipzig 1931 <PAH 1141>). [283

Due, B.: The Trial of the Generals in Xenophon's *Hellenica*. In: C&M 34, 1983, 33-44. [284

Due, B.: Lysander in Xenophon's *Hellenica*. In: C&M 38, 1987, 53-62. [285

Due, B.: The Cyropaedia : Xenophon's aims and methods. Århus, 1989. 264 pp. – Thesis <= DOAII no 350>. [286

Due, B.: The Return of Alcibiades in Xenophon's Hellenica I.IV,8-23. In: C&M 42, 1991, 39-53. [287

ZOZIMUS

Damsholt, T.: Das Zeitalter des Zozimos : Euagrios, Eustathios und die Aufhebung des chrysargyrion. In: ARID 8, 1977, 89-102. – Zozimus' *Historia nova* dated to the end of the 5th cent. [288

EPIGRAPHY

Note. A number of items of epigraphical nature can be found in the sections on Carmina Epigraphica (under AUTHORS AND TEXTS), as well as in topographical sections.

MINOAN AND MYCENEAN EPIGRAPHY

Hallager, E.: Fragments of Linear A tablets with new signs from Chania. In: AAA 5, 1972, 508-510. [289

Hallager, E.: Tablets and roundels from Khania with Linear A inscriptions. In: Kadmos 12, 1973, 20-27. [290

Hallager, E. & Pålsson, B.: A further fragment of Linear A from the Greek-Swedish excavations at Kastelli, Khania. In: AAA 8, 1975, 91-93. – On the inscription KH 79. [291

Hallager, E.: Linear A and Linear B Inscriptions from the Excavations at Kastelli, Khania 1964-1972. In: OpAth 11, 1975, 53-86. [292

Hallager, E. & Vlasakis, M.: KH Inscriptions 1976. In: AAA 9, 1976, 213-219. [293

Hallager, E.: A fragment of a Linear B tablet from Knossos. In: Kadmos 16, 1977, 24-25. – On the inscription KN X 8832. [294

Hallager, E.: Two Linear A tablets from the Greek-Swedish Excavations, Kastelli, Khania 1977. In: SMEA 19, 1978, 35-47. [295

Hallager, E.: A new Linear A inscription from Khania. In: Kadmos 19, 1980, 9-11. – On the inscription KH 90. [296

Hallager, E.: The Greek-Swedish Excavations Kastelli, Khania 1980. The Linear B Inscriptions. In: AAA 16, 1983, 58-73. [297

Blomqvist, J.: Tronsalsinventarier i Pylos. In: Medusa 7:3, 1986, 22-30. – In Swedish. [298

Hallager, E. & Vlasakis, M.: New evidence of Linear A archives from Khania. In: Kadmos 25, 1986, 108-118. [299

Hallager, E.; Vlasakis, M.; Hallager, B.P.: The First Linear B Tablet(s) from Khania. In: Kadmos 29, 1990, 24-34. [300

Hallager, E.; Vlasakis, M.; Markoulaki, S.: New and hitherto unpublished Linear A Documents from Kastelli, Khania. In: Kadmos 30, 1991, 34-41. [301

GREEK EPIGRAPHY

Bundgaard, J.A.: Le sujet de IG I^2 24. In: Mélanges helléniques offerts à George Daux. Paris, 1974, 43-49. – Proposes that the text does not refer to the Nike temenos, but to the limestone temple. [302

Hansen, P.A.: Friedländer, Epigrammata 177 d. In: ZPE 16, 1975, 79-80. – Proposes that the verb is to be read as a subjunctive form. [303

Hansen, P.A.: Review of Moretti, L.: Iscrizioni storiche ellenistiche, II ... Firenze 1976. In: CR 28, 1978, 129-130. [304

Hansen, O.: A Note on SEG 26.1422-23. In: ZPE 49, 1982, 190. [305

Hansen, O.: Some Remarks on 'Agonistische Inschrift aus Myra' (ZPE 39, 1980) and a Note on IG i^2 57; EM 6596. In: Eranos 80, 1982, 173. [306

Hansen, O.: A Geological Note on the Themistocles-Decree. In: ZPE 53, 1983, 228. – Suggests the use of Troezen marble, based on the description. [307

Hansen, O.: On the Greek graffiti at Abu Simbel concerning the campaign of Psammetichus II in Ethiopia. In: ZÄS 111, 1984, 84. [308

Hansen, O.: Some notes on inscriptions from SEG 27. In: Eranos 82, 1984, 214-215. – On SEG 27.10, 281, and 338. [309

Hansen, O.: Epigraphica varia. In: AEphem 1986, 154-159. – On inscriptions from Dreros, Sparta, Athens and Telos. [310

Hansen, O.: A Possible Variant of *Beta* in A Cyrenaic Inscription. In: Mnemosyne 39, 1986, 141-142. – On SEG 27.1176. [311

Hansen, O.: The purported letter of Darius to Gadates. In: RhM 129, 1986, 95-96. – Suggests that the inscription SIG 22 from Deirmendjik, Turkey, is based upon a forgery of 494-491/0 BC. [312

Hansen, O.: Epigraphica varia. In: Eranos 85, 1987, 99-104. – On SEG 28.440 and inscriptions from Halicarnassus, Rheneia, Pamphylia, Chiaca, and Delos. [313

Hansen, O.: On the Athenian decree concerning Salamis. In: Hermes 115, 1987, 500. – New reading suggested. [314

Hansen, O.: On the origin of a Lokrian bronze plaque concerning the settlement of new territory. In: StClas 25, 1988, 89-90. [315

Hansen, O.: The Date of the Archaic dedication of the Lacedaemonians to Olympian Zeus. In: Kadmos 29, 1990, 170. – New reading of *Paus.* V 24,3 suggested. [316

Hansen, O.: On a Corinthian epitaph from Salamis. In: AC 60, 1991, 206-207. – Re-examination of the inscription. [317

Hansen, O.: On the inscription on the Serpent Coloumn in the Hippodrome of Istanbul. In: LCM 16, 1991, 84-85. [318

LATIN EPIGRAPHY

Pedersen, F.S.: Some unpublished inscriptions from Rome or Ostia. In: ARID 9, 1980, 69-73. [319

Bruun, N.W.: Zu *CIL* IV 1618. In: C&M 39, 1988, 217-218. – New reading of the graffito on the picture Napoli, Mus.Naz. 9257 (Amore punito) from Pompeii VII 2.23. [320

Bruun, N.W.: A *penicillo?* (Tab. cer. Pomp. Année Epigr. 1973 n. 141). In: Eranos 87, 1989, 146. – Points out that the words are a researcher's note, not part of the text. [321

Almar, K.P.: Inscriptiones Latinae. Eine illustrierte Einführung in die lateinische Epigraphik (= Odense University Classical Studies 14). Odense, 1990. 569 pp. [322

PAPYROLOGY

Bülow-Jacobsen, A. & Ebbesen, S.: Five Copenhagen Papyri. In: CIMAGL 6, 1971, 41 p., 6 pls.. – On P.Haun. 24, 28, 317, 318, 406 (all of the classical period). [323

Bülow-Jacobsen, A.: Family Letter. In: ZPE 29, 1978, 253-258. – On P.Haun. inv. 16. [324

Bülow-Jacobsen, A.: Papyrus in Three Layers? P. Haun. 1 (inv. no. 5n). In: ChrÉg 53, no 105. 1978, 158-161. – Technical observations. [325

Bülow-Jacobsen, A.: Review of Archiv für Papyrusforschung und verwandte Gebiete 24-25; Leipzig 1976. In: BibO 25, 1978, 108-110. [326

Bülow-Jacobsen, A.: The Archiprophetes. In: Actes XV Congr. Intern. de papyrologie, Vol. 4. Bruxelles, 1979, 124-131. [327

Bülow-Jacobsen, A.: P. Haun. 6. An Inspection of the Original. In: ZPE 36, 1979, 91-100. [328

Bülow-Jacobsen, A.: Notice Concerning the International Photographic Archive of Papyri. In: ZPE 39, 1980, 147. – Further short reports by the author and W. van Rengen on the Archive's activities (with slight variations in titles) in ZPE 56, 1984, 139-140; 61, 1985, 33-34; 66, 1986, 99-101; 70, 1987, 63-64. (Partly relevant) [329

Bülow-Jacobsen, A.: Review of Tomsin, A.: Berliner Leihgabe griechischer Papyri II; Stockholm 1977. In: BibO 27, 1980, 53-54. [330

Bülow-Jacobsen, A.: Lease of Fishing Rights. In: Papyri, Greek & Egyptian, edited in Honour of Eric Gardner Turner (= Graeco-Roman Memoirs 68). London, 1981, 123-126. – On P. Haun. inv. 21. [331

Bülow-Jacobsen, A.: Papyri graecae Haunienses, Fasc. 2 (P. Haun. II, 13-44): Letters and mummy labels from Roman Egypt (= Papyrologische Texte und Abhandlungen 29). Kbh., 1981. xiv + 88 pp, 16 pls. (Partly relevant) [332

Bülow-Jacobsen, A. & Whitehorne, J.E.G.: The Oxyrhynchus papyri, Vol. 49 (= Graeco-Roman memoirs 69). London, 1982. 291 pp, 8 pls. [333

Bülow-Jacobsen, A.: Review of Archiv für Papyrusforschung und verwandte Gebiete Vol. 27, Leipzig 1980, and of S. Omar: Das Archiv des Sothericos (P. Soterichos), Opladen 1979. In: BibO 39, 1982, 87-89, 92-97. [334

Bülow-Jacobsen, A.: Review of Kramer, B. *et al.* (eds.): Kölner Papyri (P. Köln), 3; Opladen 1980. In: CR 32, 1982, 115-116. [335

Bülow-Jacobsen, A.: Three Ptolemaic Tax-Reciepts from Hawara (P.Carlsberg 46-48). In: BICS 29, 1982, 12-16. [336

Bülow-Jacobsen, A.: P.Carlsberg 24: Questions to an Oracle. In: ZPE 57, 1984, 91-92. – The papyrus is from the 1st cent. AD. [337

Bülow-Jacobsen, A. & Larsen, T.: Papyri graecae Haunienses, Fasc. 3 (P. Haun. III, 45-69): Subliterary texts and Byzantine documents from Egypt (= Papyrologische Texte und Abhandlungen 36). Kbh., 1985. 93 pp, 12 pls. [338

Bülow-Jacobsen, A. & McCarren, V.P.: P.Haun. 14, P.Mich. 679 and P.Haun. 15 – A Re-edition. In: ZPE 58, 1985, 71-79. – Re-edition of three papyri belonging together. [339

Bülow-Jacobsen, A.: [P.Rendel Harris] 211. Petition? In: The Rendel Harris Papyri, Vol. II. Ed. R.M. Coles *et al.* (= Studia Amstelodamensia 26). 1985, 113-114. [340

Bülow-Jacobsen, A.: Receipt for φελωχικόν (P.Carlsberg 51). In: BICS 32, 1985, 45-48. [341

Bülow-Jacobsen, A.: Orders to Arrest. P.Haun. inv. 33 and 54 and a Consolidated List. In: ZPE 66, 1986, 93-98. – The papyri are of the 2nd cent. AD. [342

Bülow-Jacobsen, A.: Review of Harrauer, H.: Griechische Texte III.2 Wien 1985. In: BibO 44, 1987, 153-155. [343

Bülow-Jacobsen, A. & el Sawy, S.: The Cairo-Preisigke Papyri, Plates (Fondation Égyptologique Reine Elisabeth). Bruxelles, 1988. 104 pp. [344

Bülow-Jacobsen, A.: Review of Fackelmann, M.: Restaurierung von Papyrus und andrere Schriftträgern aus Ägypten. Amsterdam 1985. In: JEA 75, 1989, 295-296. [345

Bülow-Jacobsen, A.: Two Greek Papyri Carlsberg from Tebtunis. P.Carlsberg 53 and 57. In: ZPE 78, 1989, 125-131. – On p. 132 a note by B. Holmen: P.Carlsberg 53 back (the verso features a drawing in Egyptian style of Khnum-Re). [346

Brashear, W.M. & Bülow-Jacobsen, A.: A Magical Formulary (P.Carlsberg 52). In: Brashear, W.M: Magica Varia (= Papyrologica Bruxellensia 25). Bruxelles, 1991, 16-62. – Greek text of a bilingual papyrus. Transcription, translation and palaeographical commentary by Bülow-Jacobsen. Note that the text may be as late as the 6th or 7th cent. [347

Bülow-Jacobsen, A.: Review of Frösén, J. & Hagedorn, D. (eds.): Die verkohlten Papyri aus Bubastos ... I, Opladen 1990. In: CR 41, 1991, 460-461. [348

PALAEOGRAPHY AND TEXTUAL CRITICISM

Note. Critical discussions of passages in an author should be sought under AUTHORS AND TEXTS.

Smith, O.L.: Two Manuscripts Identified as One. Parma 154 + Par. Gr. 2821. In: Mnemosyne 27, 1974, 414-415. – Proposes that the mss were originally parts of the same codex. [349

Smith, O.L.: A note on Holkham Gr. 88 and Marc. Gr. 622. In: Maia 27, 1975, 205. – Demonstrates that the two mss (Aristophanes and Hesych, respectively) are in the same hand. [350

Smith, O.L.: Tricliniana. In: C&M 33, 1981/82, 239-262. [351

Smith, O.L.: Anonymus Mutinensis or Andronikos Kallistos? In: C&M 37, 1986, 255-258. – On the question of one or two scribal hands in the mss attributed to Kallistos <cf. No 351, pp. 256-258>. [352

Lund, A.A.: Prinzipielle Bemerkungen zur höheren Textkritik. In: Hermes 117, 1989, 204-210. – The examples are drawn from Seneca *Cons. ad Marciam*. [353

See also no 229

MANUSCRIPTS IN COPENHAGEN

Schartau, B. & Smith, O.L.: Towards a descriptive catalogue of the Greek manuscripts of the Royal Library, Copenhagen. In: Scriptorium 28, 1974, 332-338. (Partly relevant) [354

LANGUAGE

Madvig, J.N.: Sprachtheoretische Abhandlungen. Herausgeb. von Karsten Friis Johansen. Kbh., 1971. 493 pp. – Pp. 1-41 introduction by Friis Johansen on Madvig's theory of language. The selected texts include on pp. 258-305: "Zerstreute sprachwissenschaftlice Bemerkungen" <PAH no 1250, orig. publ. in Kleine philologische Schriften, Leipzig 1875 <PAH no 3205>>; on pp. 327-336 excerpts from: "Bemerkungen über verschiedene Puncte des Systems der lateinischen Sprachlehre und einige Einzelheiten derselben", orig. publ. Braunschweig 1843 <PAH no 1386>, and on pp. 393-397 the preface to: "Kleine philologische Schriften". [355

GREEK LANGUAGE

Blomqvist, J.: Grekiska dialekter i mykensk tid. In: MT 48-51, 1982, 5-20. [356

Blomqvist, J.: Translation Greek in the trilingual inscription of Xanthus. In: OpAth 14, 1982, 11-20. – On mid-4th cent. BC translation technique. [357

GREEK ETYMOLOGY AND LEXICOGRAPHY
Mejer, J.: A note on the word ἀκέφαλος. In: C&M 32, 1971/80 [1980], 127-131. [358

Hansen, M.H.: The Origin of the Term Demokratia. In: LCM 11, 1986, 35-36. – Notes that the word exists ab. 470 BC. [359

Hansen, O.: The king-title βασιλίσκος in Nubia in the fourth to sixth century A.D. In: JEA 72, 1986, 205. [360

Hansen, O.: The etymology of Greek σταφυλῖνος "carrot". In: HSF 102, 1989, 211. [361

Hansen, O.: Οὐρανός and Sanskrit Varuṇa. In: Eranos 88, 1990, 162. [362

GREEK PHONOLOGY
Schartau, B.: 'Mini-Gloss' or Variant? In: CIMAGL 48, 1984, 149-162. – On Attic h over Doric a in Byzantine mss of the dramatists; Euripides is used as a test-case. [363

Rasmussen, J.E.: Zur Abbauhierachie des Nasalpräsens – vernehmlich im Arischen und Griechischen. In: Sprachwissenschaft und Philologie : Jacob Wackernagel und die Indogermanistik heute. Ed. H. Eichner & H. Rix. Wiesbaden, 1990, 188-201. (Partly relevant) [364

GREEK SYNTAX
Blomqvist, J.: On adversative coordination in ancient Greek and as a universal linguistic phaenomenon. In: ActaSLU III,2, 1981, 57-70. [365

Tortzen, C.G.: Male and Female in Peripatetic Botany. In: C&M 42, 1991, 81-110. – On the use of gender in referring to plants. [366

LATIN LANGUAGE

LATIN ETYMOLOGY AND LEXICOGRAPHY
Wiese, C.F.: s.v. iaculum – iaculus, idcirco, identidem – identitas, idoneitas – idonitas, ignarures – ignarus. In: TLL VII 1 (fasc. 1-2), 1934, 1935, cols. 74-79, 172-178, 210-212, 229-238, 271-276. [367

Hastrup, T.: s.v. hernia – herniosus, hiatus, hio, hirnea – hirniola. In: TLL VI 3 (fasc. 14-15), 1937, 1938, cols. 2658-2659, 2681-2684, 2810-2813, 2823. [367a

Nielsen, P.W.: s.v. intempestive – intemporalitas, intendo – intente, intentio, intercalaris – intercapito, interceptio – interceptus, intercilium – intercipio. In: TLL VII 1 (fasc. 14), 1963, cols. 2109-2111, 2112-2119, 2120-2122, 2150-2153, 2157-2158, 2163-2167. [368

Krarup, P.: Review of Tiisala, Y.: Die griechischen Lehnwörter bei den römischen Historikeren ... Jyväskylä 1974. In: Gnomon 49, 1977, 515-516. [369

Friis-Jensen, K.: Beiträge aus der Thesaurus-Arbeit XXII: Praedurare and perdurare as gastronomic terms. In: MH 41, 1984, 39-42. [370

Friis-Jensen, K.: s.v. Praeduratio – praedure, praemo – praeemptor, praefectualis, praefecturalis – praefensior, praefestinatim – praefestinus, praefidens – praefido, praefluo – praefluus, praeingens – praelabor, praelectio – praelego, praeligamen – praeligo, praenao – praenavigo. In: TLL X, 2 (fasc. 4-5), 1985, 1987, cols. 592-594, 604-605, 609, 618-619, 633, 645-646, 672-683, 686-689, 691-692, 729. [371

Bruun, N.W.: s.v. Praeordinatio, praeordino. In: TLL X, 2 (fasc. 5), 1987, 747-748. [372

Nielsen, H.S.: *Alumnus*: A Term of Relation Denoting Quasi-Adoption. In: C&M 38, 1987, 141-188. [373

Nielsen, H.S.: On the Use of the Terms of Relation "Mamma" and "Tata" in the Epitaphs of CIL VI. In: C&M 40, 1989, 191-196. [374

Bruun, N.W.: s.v. Pastura – pastus (-i), patriarcha – patriarchius, patrimonialis – patrimonius, patulus, pausa – pauso, peculiaris – peculium. In: TLL X, 1 (fasc. 5-6), 1990, 1991, cols. 647-651, 742-744, 750-756, 794-797, 856-861, 922-933. [375

Nielsen, H.S.: *Delicia* in Roman Literature and in the Urban Inscriptions. In: ARID 19, 1990, 79-88. [376

Hansen, O.: The Province, not the Island of Sicily. In: Latomus 50, 1991, 184.
– Suggests that the Latin concept of the word focuses on Sicily's status as a province, ignoring the geographical aspect. [377

Nielsen, H.S.: Ditis Examen Domus? On the Use of the Term *Verna* in the Roman Epigraphical and Literary Sources. In: C&M 42, 1991, 221-240. [378

LATIN PHONOLOGY
Lauritsen, J.: Word Final Velar and Labial Stops in Latin. In: Glotta 56, 1978, 94-98. [379

HISTORY OF LITERATURE

Nøjgaard, M.: Review of Pugliarello, M.: Le origini della favolistica classica. Brescia 1973. In: Gnomon 49, 1977, 413-415. [380

Nøjgaard, M.: La moralisation de la fable, d'Ésope à Romulus. In: La fable. Huit exposés suivis de discussions. Ed. F. Rodríguez Adrados. (= Entretiens Hardt 30). Genéve, 1983, 225-251. [381

Mejer, J. & Skafte Jensen, M.: Litteraturens historia. Vol. I: Forntiden. Stockholm, 1985. 398 pp. – Translation of Oldtiden. Kbh., 1985 <DOAII no 434>. [382

Mejer, J. & Skafte Jensen, M.: Verdens litteraturhistorie. Vol. I: Oldtiden. Oslo, 1985. 398 pp. – Translation of Oldtiden <cf. no 382>. [383

Nøjgaard, M.: Review of Adrados, F.R.: Historia de la fábula greco-latina I-II. Madrid 1979. In: Gnomon 58, 1986, 193-198. [384

Thomsen, M.-L.: The Wisdom of the Chaldaeans. Mesopotamian Magic as Concieved by Classical Authors. In: East and West <no 1180>, 1988, 93-101. [385

HISTORY OF GREEK LITERATURE

Bendz, G.: Den grekiska litteraturen. In: Litteraturens världs historia; Vol. I: Forntiden. Stockholm, 1971, 201-409. – Translation of Den græske litteratur. Kbh., 1971 <DOAI no 476>. [386

Bendz, G.: Gresk litteratur. In: Verdens litteraturhistorie, Vol. I: Oldtiden. Oslo, 1971, 211-428. – Translation of Den græske litteratur <cf. no 386>. [387

Friis Johansen, H.: Review of Kaimio, M.: The Chorus of Greek Drama ... Helsinki 1970. In: Gnomon 46, 1974, 4-9. [388

Andersen, L.: Studies in oracular verses. Concordance to Delphic responses in hexameter. Kbh., 1987. xx + 274 pp. [389

Andersen, L.: Greek Epic and Greek Mythology and their Links with The Near East. In: East and West <no 1180>, 1988, 33-43. [390

Lund, A.A.: Review of Herrmann, J. (ed.): Griechische und lateinische Quellen zur Frühgeschichte ..., I: Von Homer bis Plutarch ... Berlin 1988. In: Klio 72, 1990, 270-273. [391

HISTORY OF LATIN LITERATURE

Bendz, G.: Den romerska litteraturen. In: Litteraturens världs historia; Vol. I <cf. no 386>, 1971, 410-563. – Translation of Den romerske litteratur. Kbh., 1971 <DOAI no 488>. [392

Bendz, G.: Romersk litteratur. In: Verdens litteraturhistorie; Vol. I <cf. no 387>, 1971, 429-592. – Translation of Den romerske litteratur <cf. no 392>. [393

Munk Olsen, B.: Les classiques latins dans les florilèges médiévaux au XIIIe siècle. In: RHT 9, 1979, 47-121. (Marginally relevant) [394

Munk Olsen, B.: Les classiques latins dans les florilèges médiévaux antérieurs au XIIIe siècle, II. In: RHT 10, 1980, 115-164. (Marginally relevant) [395

Munk Olsen, B.: L'étude des auteurs classiques latins aux XIe et XIIe siècles. Vol. 1-3:2. Paris, 1982, 1985, 1987, 1989. xxxii + 597, xvi + 886, xi + 379, xv + 292 pp. (Partly relevant) [396

Christensen, T.: The So-called *Appendix* to Eusebius' *Historia Ecclesiastica* VIII. In: C&M 34, 1983, 177-209. – Points to the existence of a pagan, pro-Constantian historical source on the tetrarchy and its aftermath until 312. [397

Grønkjær, N.: Agostino e la retorica romana. In: ARID 14, 1985, 149-161. (Partly relevant) [398

Lund, A.A.: Zur Schilderung der Germanischen Gesellschaft bei Caesar und Tacitus. In: C&M 36, 1985, 177-197. [399

HISTORY

GENERAL, POLITICAL, AND LEGAL HISTORY
Hyldahl, N.: s.v. Hinrichtung (Sections A; BIa; BIIa; C). In: Reallexikon für Antike und Christentum 15, 1989, cols. 342-351, 356-357, 362-364. [400

SOCIAL, ECONOMIC, AND CULTURAL HISTORY
Skydsgaard, J.E.: Review of Finley, M.I.: The Ancient Economy. Berkeley 1973. In: T&C 16, 1975, 617-619. [401

Skydsgaard, J.E.: L'agricoltura greca e romana: tradizioni a confronto. In: ARID 16, 1987, 7-24. [402

Randsborg, K.: Between Classical antiquity and the Middle Ages : new evidence of economic change. In: Antiquity 64, 1990, 122-127. (Partly relevant) [403

GREEK HISTORY

GREEK GENERAL, POLITICAL AND LEGAL HISTORY
Hansen, O.: An attic drinking-song as a possible source for Peisistratus' campaign for the possession of Sigeum in the Troad. In: PP 42, 1987, 108-109. [404

Meyer, J.C.: Archaic Greece : A Case of Ancient "Modernization"? In: Studies ... <no 1181>, 1988, 39-49. [405

GREEK SOCIAL, ECONOMIC, AND CULTURAL HISTORY

Skydsgaard, J.E.: Transhumance in ancient Greece. In: Pastoral economics in classical antiquity. Ed. C.R. Whitaker (= Proceed. of the Cambridge Philological Society, Supplement 14). Cambridge, 1988, 75-86. [406

Grinder-Hansen, K.: Charon's Fee in Ancient Greece? Some Remarks on a Well-known Death Rite. In: Recent Danish Research ... <no 793>, 1991, 207-218. [407

ETRUSCAN HISTORY

Strøm, I.: Aspetti delle aristocrazie fra VIII e VII sec. a.C. Problemi riguardanti l'influsso dei paesi mediterranei sulla formazione delle città etrusche e il ruolo delle aristocrazie. In: Opus 3, 1984, 355-365. [408

Nielsen, M.: Women in the Late Etruscan Society : Practices of Commemoration and Social Stress. In: Festskrift til Thelma Jexlev: Fromhed og verdslighed i middelalder og renaissance. Odense, 1985, 192-202. [409

Rathje, A.: Manners and Customs in Central Italy in the Orientalizing Period: Influence from the Near East. In: East and West <no 1180>, 1988, 81-90. [410

Nielsen, M.: La donna e la famiglia nella tarda società etrusca. In: Le Donne in Etruria. Ed. A. Rallo. Roma, 1989, 121-145. [411

Nielsen, M.: Women and Family in a Changing Society : a Quantitative Approach to Late Etruscan Burials. In: ARID 17/18, 1989, 53-98. [412

Hansen, O.: The Coins with the Legend MEP and the Origin of the Etruscans. In: PP 45, 1990, 447-448. [413

Nielsen, M.: Sacerdotesse e associazioni cultuali femminili in Etruria : testimonianze epigrafiche ed iconografiche. In: ARID 19, 1990, 45-67. [414

Rathje, A.: The Adoption of the Homeric Banquet in Central Italy in the Orientalizing Period. In: Sympotica : A Symposium on the Symposion. Ed. O. Murray. Oxford, 1990, 279-288. [415

Rathje, A.: Il banchetto presso i fenici. In: Atti II Congr. Intern. di Studi Fenici e Punici, Roma 1987. Roma, 1991, 1165-1168. (Marginally relevant) [416

ROMAN HISTORY

ROMAN GENERAL AND POLITICAL HISTORY

Isager, J.: Vespasiano e Augusto. In: Studia Romana ... <no 1177>, 1976, 64-71. – On Vespasian's imitations of Augustus. [417

Bilde, P.: The Roman Emperor Gaius (Caligula)'s Attempt to Erect his Statue in the Temple of Jerusalem. In: STh 32, 1978, 67-93. [418

Christensen, T.: The so-called Edict of Milan. In: C&M 35, 1984, 129-175. – English version of Det såkaldte Milanoedikt, published in DTT 37, 1974. [419

Hedeager, L.: Empire, frontier and the babarian hinterland : Rome and Northern Europe from 1-400 AD. In: Centre and Periphery in the Ancient World. Ed. by M. Rowlands, M. Larsen and K. Kristiansen. Cambridge, 1987, 125-140. (Partly relevant) [420

Houby-Nielsen, S.: Augustus and the Hellenistic Kings. A Note on the Augustan Propaganda. In: East and West <no 1180>, 1988, 116-128. [421

Nedergaard, E.: The Four Sons of Phraates IV in Rome. In: East and West <no 1180>, 1988, 102-115. [422

Ørsted, P.: *Regiones Italiae*, Ehreninschriften und Imperialpolitik. In: Studies ... <no 1181>, 1988, 124-138. [423

ROMAN CONSTITUTIONAL AND ADMINISTRATIVE HISTORY

Malcus, B.: Senaten i romersk historia och tradition. In: HT 1972, 317-354. [424

Thomsen, R.: The Pay of the Roman Soldier and the Property Qualifications of the Servian Classes. In: Classica ... <no 1176>, 1973, 194-208. [425

Pedersen, F.S.: Late Roman Public Professionalism (= Odense University Classical Studies 9). Odense, 1976. 88 pp.. – On the existence and scope of official policy in Late Roman public administration. Also printed, due to editorial confusion, in C&M 31, 1970 [1975], 161-213 with the title: On Professional Qualifications for Public Posts in Late Antiquity. [426

Thomsen, R.: The Servian Census Classes and Roman Coinage. In: Actes VIII Congr. Intern. de Numismatique, New York-Washington septembre 1973. Paris/Bâle, 1976, 377-381. [427

Ørsted, P.: Roman Imperial Economy and Romanization. A study in Roman imperial administration and the public lease system in the Danubian provinces from the first to the third century A.D. Kbh., 1985. 415 pp, 2 pls. – Thesis <= DOAII no 711>. [428

Meyer, J.C.: From a Turkish village to republican Rome. Ideology, mentality and control. In: Staat und Staatlichkeit in der frühen römischen Republik. Akten eines Symposiums, 12.-15. Juli 1988, Freie Universität Berlin. Ed. W. Eder. Stuttgart, 1990, 258-277. [429

ROMAN SOCIAL, ECONOMIC, AND CULTURAL HISTORY
Skydsgaard, J.E.: Transhumance in Ancient Italy. In: ARID 7, 1974, 7-36. [430

Skydsgaard, J.E.: The Disintegration of the Roman Labour Market and the Clientela Theory. In: Studia Romana ... <no 1177>, 1976, 44-48. – Paper read on the 6th Intern. Congr. on Economic History, Copenhagen 1974. [431

Skydsgaard, J.E.: Non-slave labour in rural Italy during the late Republic. In: Non-slave Labour in the Graeco-Roman World. Ed. P. Garnsey. Cambridge, 1980, 65-72. [432

Wanscher, O.: Sella Curulis : The folding stool. An ancient symbol of dignity. Kbh., 1980. 350 pp. [433

Skydsgaard, J.E.: Public Building and Society. In: Città e architettura ... <no 668>, 1983, 223-227. – On public building as an economic factor, exemplified by the Colosseum. [434

Bekker-Nielsen, T.: Terra Incognita: the Subjective Geography of the Roman Empire. In: Studies ... <no 1181>, 1988, 148-161. [435

Saxtorph, N.M.: The Emperor's Men. In: Studies ... <no 1181>, 1988, 162-165. – On social mobility in the Principate. [436

Tvarnø, H.: Roman Social Structure : Different Approaches for Different Purposes. In: Studies ... <no 1181>, 1988, 114-123. [437

Lund, A.A.: Zum Germanenbild der Römer: Eine Einführung in die antike Ethnographie. Heidelberg, 1990. iv + 100 pp. [438

Carlsen, J.: Estate management in Roman North Africa. Transformation or continuity? In: L'Africa romana 8, 1991, 625-637. [439

Poulsen, B.: The Dioscuri and ruler ideology. In: SymbOsl 66, 1991, 119-146. [440

BIOGRAPHY

Note. Items of a partially biographical nature are listed in the historical sections.

Thomsen, R.: King Servius Tullius : a historical synthesis (= Humanitas 5). Kbh., 1980. 347 pp. [441

Mørkholm, O.: Antiochus IV. In: The Cambridge History of Judaism, Vol. II. Cambridge, 1989, 278-291. – The manuscript was originally submitted 1970; some changes were made before the author's death in 1983. [442

TOPOGRAPHY

Note. The topographical section is subdivided as follows: GREECE; ITALY AND SICILY; EUROPE OUTSIDE GREECE AND ITALY; ASIA MINOR; CYPRUS, SYRIA AND PALESTINE;

OTHER AREAS OF ASIA; AFRICA. Each subsection is further subdived by regions (alphabetically arranged) and – if ten or more items are listed under the region – by cities.

The section contains historical and archaeological items concerned with one particular locality. Exempted from this are items of POTTERY and NUMISMATICS, for which see those sections.

GREECE

Archaeology in the Dodecanese. Eds. S. Dietz and I. Papachristodoulou. Kbh., 1988. 260 pp. [443

ARGOLIS
Dietz, S.: A Bronze Age Tumulus Cemetery in Asine, Southern Greece. In: Archaeology 28, 1975, 157-163. – The article is sometimes quoted as A Middle Helladic Tumulus ... [444

Dietz, S. & Styrenius, C.-G.: Asine [1971]. In: ADelt 27, 1972 [1976], Chron. 231-233. [445

Styrenius, C.G. et al.: Asine. Barbouna area. In: ADelt 28, 1973 [1977], Chron. 155-159. [446

Rafn, B.: Asine II : Results of the Excavations East of the Acropolis 1970-1974. Fasc. 6: The Post-Geometric Periods: Part 1: The Graves of the Early Fifth Century B.C. (= SkrAth 24:6.1). Stockholm, 1979. 30 pp. [447

Dietz, S.: Asine II : Results of the Excavations East of the Acropolis 1970-1974. Fasc. 2: The Middle Helladic cemetery, the Middle Helladic and Early Mycenean deposits (= SkrAth 24:2). Stockholm, 1980. 144 pp. [448

Dietz, S.: Asine II : Results of the Excavations East of the Acropolis 1970-1974. Fasc. 1: General stratigraphical analysis and architectural remains (= SkrAth 24:1). Stockholm, 1982. 144 pp. [449

Dietz, S.: Kontinuität und Kulturwende in der Argolis von 2000-700 v.Chr. Ergebnisse der neuen schwedisch-dänischen Ausgrabungen in Asine. In: Zur ägäischen Frühzeit (= Kleine Schriften aus dem Vorgeschichtlichen Seminar Marburg 17), 1984, 23-52. [450

Hansen, O.: Some possible evidence for an Amphictiony in Tiryns. In: AAA 17, 1984, 162-163. [451

Rafn, B.: The Ritual Use of Pottery in the Nekropolis at Halieis. In: Ancient Greek and Related Pottery. Proceed. of the Intern. Vase Symposium in Amsterdam 12-15 April 1984; Ed. H.A.G. Brijder. Amsterdam, 1984, 305-308. [452

Strøm, I.: The so-called altar above the shaft grave IV at Mycenae. In: AArch 54, 1983 [1985], 141-146. [453

Strøm, I.: The early sanctuary of the Argive Heraion and its external relations (8th-early 6th cent. B.C.) : the monumental architecture. In: AArch 59, 1988 [1989], 173-203. [454

Dietz, S. & Divari-Valakou, N.: A Middle Helladic III/Late Helladic I grave group from Myloi in the Argolid (Oikopedon Manti). In: OpAth 18, 1990, 45-62. [455

Dietz, S.: The Argolid at the Transition to the Mycenaean Age. Studies in the Chronology and Cultural Development in the Shaft Grave Period. Kbh., 1991. 336 pp. – Thesis <= DOAII no 927>. [456

Rafn, B.: Archaic and Classical Graves at Haleis : A Summary. In: Recent Danish Research ... <no 793>, 1991, 57-71. [457

ATTICA
1. Historical subjects

Thomsen, R.: The Origin of Ostracism : A Synthesis (= Humanitas 4). Kbh., 1972. 158 pp. [458

Damsgaard-Madsen, A.: Le mode de désignation des démarques attiques au quatrième siècle avant J.-C.. In: Classica ... <no 1176>, 1973, 92-118. [459

Hansen, M.H.: The Sovereignty of the People's Court in Athens in the Fourth Century B. C. and The Public Action against Unconstitutional Proposals (= Odense University Classical Studies 4). Odense, 1974. 80 pp. [460

Hansen, M.H.: *Eisangelia* : The Sovereignty of the People's Court in Athens in the Fourth Century B. C. and the Impeachment of Generals and Politicians (= Odense University Classical Studies 6). Odense, 1975. 136 pp. [461

Isager, S. & Hansen, M.H.: Aspects of Athenian Society in the Fourth Century B. C. : A historical introduction to and commentary on the *paragraphe*-speeches and the speech *Against Dionysodorus* in the *Corpus Demosthenicum* (XXXII-XXXVIII and LVI) (= Odense University Classical Studies 5). Odense, 1975. 270 pp. – Revised English version of the introduction and commentaries of: Attiske Retstaler, Kbh. 1972 <DOAI no 173>. [462

Hansen, M.H.: *Apagoge, Endeixis* and *Ephegesis* against *Kakourgoi, Atimoi* and *Pheugontes* : A Study in the Athenian Administration of Justice in the Fourth Century B.C. (= Odense University Classical Studies 8). Odense, 1976. 171 pp. – Revised English version of thesis: Atimistraffen i klassisk tid, Kbh., 1973 <DOAI no 597>. [463

Hansen, M.H.: How Many Athenians Attended the *Ecclesia*? In: GRBS 17, 1976, 115-134. – Repr. with addenda in: The Athenian Ecclesia <no 490>, 1-23. [464

Hansen, M.H.: The Theoric Fund and the *graphe paranomon* against Apollodorus. In: GRBS 17, 1976, 235-246. [465

Hansen, M.H.: How Did the Athenian *Ecclesia* Vote? In: GRBS 18, 1977, 123-137. – Repr. with addenda in: The Athenian Ecclesia <no 490>, 103-121. [466

Hansen, M.H.: How Often Did the *Ecclesia* Meet? In: GRBS 18, 1977, 43-70. – Repr. with addenda in: The Athenian Ecclesia <no 490>, 35-72. [467

Thomsen, R.: War in Classical Athens. In: Armées et Fiscalité dans la Monde antique: Colloques Nationaux de CNRS no 936. Paris, 1977, 135-147. [468

Hansen, M.H.: *Demos*, *Ecclesia* and *Dicasterion* in Classical Athens. In: GRBS 19, 1978, 127-146. – Repr. with addenda in: The Athenian Ecclesia <no 490>, 139-160. [469

Hansen, M.H.: *Nomos* and *Psephisma* in Fourth-Century Athens. In: GRBS 19, 1978, 315-330. – Repr. with addenda in: The Athenian Ecclesia <no 490>, 161-177. [470

Hansen, M.H.: Οἱ προέδροι τῶν νομοθετῶν. A Note on IG II² 222, 41-52. In: ZPE 30, 1978, 151-157. [471

Hansen, M.H.: Did the Athenian *Ecclesia* Legislate after 403/2 B.C.? In: GRBS 20, 1979, 27-53. – Repr. with addenda in: The Athenian Ecclesia <no 490>, 179-206. [472

Hansen, M.H.: The Duration of a Meeting of the Athenian Ecclesia. In: CP 74, 1979, 43-49. – Repr. with addenda in: The Athenian Ecclesia <no 490>, 131-138. [473

Hansen, M.H.: Ἐκκλησία σύγκλητος in Hellenistic Athens. In: GRBS 20, 1979, 149-156. – Repr. with addenda in: The Athenian Ecclesia <no 490>, 73-81. [474

Hansen, M.H.: How Often Did the Athenian *Dicasteria* Meet? In: GRBS 20, 1979, 243-246. [475

Hansen, M.H.: Misthos for Magistrates in Classical Athens. In: SymbOsl 54, 1979, 5-22. [476

Hansen, M.H.: Athenian *Nomothesia* in the Fourth Century B.C. and Demosthenes' Speech against Leptines. In: C&M 32, 1971/80 [1980], 87-104. [477

Hansen, M.H.: *Eisangelia* in Athens : A Reply. In: JHS 100, 1980, 89-95. [478

Hansen, M.H.: Perquisites for magistrates in fourth-century Athens. In: C&M 32, 1971/80 [1980], 105-125. [479

Hansen, M.H.: Seven Hundred *Archai* in Classical Athens. In: GRBS 21, 1980, 151-173. [480

Gabrielsen, V.: Remuneration of State Officials in the Fourth Century B.C. Athens (= Odense University Classical Studies 11). Odense, 1981. 165 pp. [481

Hansen, M.H.: Demographic Reflections on the Number of Athenian Citizens 451-309 B.C. In: AJAH 7, 1981, 172-189. [482

Hansen, M.H.: Initiative and Decision : The Separation of Powers in Fourth-Century Athens. In: GRBS 22, 1981, 345-370. [483

Hansen, M.H.: The Number of Athenian Hoplites in 431 B.C. In: SymbOsl 56, 1981, 19-32. [484

Hansen, M.H.: The Prosecution of Homicide in Athens: A Reply. In: GRBS 22, 1981, 11-30. [485

Hansen, M.H.: The Athenian *Heliaia* from Solon to Aristotele. In: C&M 33, 1981/82, 9-47. – Repr. with addenda in: The Athenian Ecclesia 2 <no 530>, 219-261. [486

Hansen, M.H.: *IG* II_ 412 : A Fragment of a Fourth-Century Athenian Law. In: C&M 33, 1981/82, 119-123. [487

Hansen, M.H.: Atimia in Consequence of Private Debts. In: Symposion 1977. Vorträge zur griechischen und hellenistischen Rechtsgeschichte. Eds. J. Modrzejewski & D. Liebs (= AGR 3). Köln, 1982, 113-120. [488

Hansen, M.H.: When Did the Athenian *Ecclesia* Meet? In: GRBS 23, 1982, 331-350. – Repr. with addenda in: The Athenian Ecclesia <no 490>, 83-102. [489

Hansen, M.H.: The Athenian Ecclesia : A Collection of Articles 1976-1983 (= Opuscula Graecolatina 26). Kbh., 1983. ix + 245 pp. [490

Hansen, M.H.: The Athenian *Ecclesia* and the Swiss *Landsgemeinde*. In: The Athenian Ecclesia <no 490>, 1983, 207-226. [491

Hansen, M.H.: The Athenian 'Politicians' 403-322 B.C. In: GRBS 24, 1983, 33-55. – Repr. with addenda in: The Athenian Ecclesia 2 <no 530>, 1-24. [492

Hansen, M.H.: *Graphe* or *Dike Traumatos*? In: GRBS 24, 1983, 301-320. [493

Hansen, M.H.: Initiative und Entscheidigung. Überlegungen über die Gewaltenteilung in Athen des 4.Jahrhunderts (= Xenia 6). Konstanz, 1983. 36 pp. – Revised German version of Initiative ... <no 483>. [494

Hansen, M.H.: Political Activity and the Organization of Attica in the Fourth Century B.C. In: GRBS 24, 1983, 227-238. – Repr. with addenda in: The Athenian Ecclesia 2 <no 530>, 73-91. [495

Hansen, M.H.: The *Procheirotonia* in the Athenian *Ecclesia*. In: The Athenian Ecclesia <no 490>, 1983, 123-130. [496

Hansen, M.H.: *Rhetores* and *Strategoi* in Fourth-Century Athens. In: GRBS 24, 1983, 149-180. – Repr. with addendum: Updated Inventory of *Rhetores* and *Strategoi* (1988), in: The Athenian Ecclesia 2 <no 530>, 25-72. [497

Hansen, M.H.: The Sovereignty of the People's Court in Athens. In: The Western Idea of Law. Toronto, 1983, 304-308. – Excerpt of Sovereignty ... <no 460>. [498

Hansen, M.H.: Two Notes on the Athenian *Dikai Emporikai*. In: Symposion 1979. Vorträge zur griechischen und hellenistischen Rechtsgeschichte. Ed. P. Dimakis (= AGR 4). Köln, 1983, 104-111. [499

Hansen, M.H.: Die athenische Volksversammlung im Zeitalter des Demosthenes. Konstanz, 1984. 211 pp. [500

Hansen, M.H. & Mitchel, F.: The Number of Ecclesiai in Fourth-Century Athens. In: SymbOsl 59, 1984, 13-19. – Repr. with addenda in: The Athenian Ecclesia 2 <no 530>, 167-175. [501

Hansen, M.H.: The Number of *Rhetores* in the Athenian *Ecclesia* 355-322 B.C. In: GRBS 25, 1984, 123-155. – Repr. with addenda in: The Athenian Ecclesia 2 <no 530>, 93-127. [502

Hansen, M.V.: Athenian Maritime Trade in the 4th Century B.C. : Operation and Finance. In: C&M 35, 1984, 71-92. [503

Gabrielsen, V.: The *Naukrariai* and the Athenian Navy. In: C&M 36, 1985, 21-51. [504

Hansen, M.H.: Athenian *Nomothesia*. In: GRBS 26, 1985, 345-371. [505

Hansen, M.H.: Review Article: The History of the Athenian Constitution [Review of Rhodes, P.J.: A Commentary on the Aristotelean "Athenaion Politeia", Oxford 1981]. In: CP 80, 1985, 51-66. [506

Hansen, O.: On the Date for an Athenian Festival. In: Mnemosyne 38, 1985, 389-390. – Inscr. given by F.W. Walbank, in Kokalos 1968-69, 476-498 dated to 329/28. [507

Vestergaard, T. *et al.*: A Typology of the Women Recorded on Gravestones from Attica. In: AJAH 19, 1985, 178-190. [508

Gabrielsen, V.: Φανερά and ἀφανὴς οὐσία in Classical Athens. In: C&M 37, 1986, 99-114. [509

Hansen, M.H.: Demography and democracy : the number of Athenian citizens in the fourth century B.C. Herning, 1986. 116 pp. – Summary published in: Proceed. of the Classical Association, London, 1986, 16-17. [510

Hansen, M.H.: Κλήρωσις ἐκ προκρίτων in Fourth-Century Athens. In: CP 81, 1986, 222-229. [511

Gabrielsen, V.: The *Antidosis* Procedure in Classical Athens. In: C&M 38, 1987, 7-38. [512

Gabrielsen, V.: The *Diadikasia*-Documents. In: C&M 38, 1987, 39-51. [513

Hansen, M.H.: The Athenian assembly in the age of Demosthenes. Oxford, 1987. viii + 249 pp. – A revised and augmented English version of Die athenische Volksversammlung ... <no 500>. [514

Hansen, M.H.: An Attic Decree of 347/6? (Peek, *Kerameikos* III No. 1). In: C&M 38, 1987, 75-79. [515

Hansen, M.H.: Did Kleisthenes Use the Lot When Trittyes were Allocated to Tribes? In: AncW 15, 1987, 43-44. [516

Hansen, M.H.: *Graphe Paranomon* against *Psephismata* not yet passed by the *Ecclesia*. In: C&M 38, 1987, 63-73. – Repr. in: The Athenian Ecclesia 2 <no 530>, 271-281. [517

Hansen, M.H.: How Often Did the Athenian *Ekklesia* Meet? A Reply. In: GRBS 28, 1987, 35-50. – Reply to E.M.Harris in CQ 36, 1986, 363-377. Repr. with addenda in: The Athenian Ecclesia 2 <no 530>, 177-194. [518

Hansen, M.H.: *Rhetores* and *Strategoi*: *Addenda et Corrigenda*. In: GRBS 28, 1987, 209-211. – Incorporated in The Athenian Ecclesia 2 <no 530>, 34-64. [519

See also no 314

Damsgaard-Madsen, A.: Attic Funeral Inscriptions : Their Use as Historical Sources and some Preliminary Results. In: Studies ... <no 1181>, 1988, 55-68. [520

Gabrielsen, V.: A Naval Debt and the Appointment of a Syntrierarch in *IG* II 2, 1623. In: C&M 39, 1988, 63-87. [521

Hansen, M.H.: The Athenian Board of Generals. When was Tribal Representation Replaced by Election from all Athenians ? In: Studies ... <no 1181>, 1988, 69-70. [522

Hansen, M.H.: The Average Age of Athenian *Bouleutai* and the proportion of *Bouleutoi* who served twice. In: LCM 13, 1988, 67-69. [523

Hansen, M.H.: Demography and Democracy Once again. In: ZPE 75, 1988, 189-193. – Comments on E. Ruschenbusch in ZPE 72, 1988. [524

Hansen, M.H.: The Organization of the Athenian Assembly. A Reply. In: GRBS 29, 1988, 51-58. – Repr. with addenda in: The Athenian Ecclesia 2 <no 530>, 155-165. [525

Hansen, M.H.: Three Studies in Athenian Demography (= HistFilosMed 56). Kbh., 1988. 28 pp. [526

Skydsgaard, J.E.: Solon's *Tele* and the Agrarian History. In: Studies ... <no 1181>, 1988, 50-54. – On the landed property qualifications for membership of a telos. [527

Gabrielsen, V.: IG II^2 1609 and Eisphora Payments in Kind? In: ZPE 79, 1989, 93-99. [528

Gabrielsen, V.: The Number of Athenian Trierarchs after ca. 340 B.C. In: C&M 40, 1989, 145-159. [529

Hansen, M.H.: The Athenian Ecclesia 2 : A Collection of Articles 1983-1989 (= Opuscula Graecolatina 31). Kbh., 1989. 324 pp. [530

Hansen, M.H.: Demography and Democracy : A Reply to Eberhard Ruschenbusch. In: AHB 3, 1989, 40-44. [531

Hansen, M.H.: *Demos, Ekklesia*, and *Dikasterion* : A Reply to Martin Ostwald and Josiah Ober. In: C&M 40, 1989, 101-106. – Repr. in: The Athenian Ecclesia 2 <no 530>, 213-218. [532

Hansen, M.H.: On the Importance of Institutions in an analysis of Athenian Democracy. In: C&M 40, 1989, 107-113. – Repr. in: The Athenian Ecclesia 2 <no 530>, 263-269. [533

Hansen, M.H.: Review Article: Athenian Democracy. Institutions and Ideology. In: CP 84, 1989, 137-148. – Review of Bleicken, J.: Die athenische Demokratie. Paderborn 1985. [534

Hansen, M.H.: Review of Sealey, R.: The Athenian Republic ... University Park, Pa. 1987. In: Gnomon 61, 1989, 744-746. [535

Hansen, M.H.: Review of Sinclair, R.K.: Democracy and Participation in Athens. Cambridge 1988. In: CR 39, 1989, 69-76. [536

Hansen, M.H.: Solonian Democracy in Fourth-Century Athens. In: C&M 40, 1989, 71-99. – Paper presented at the conference "Athenian Democracy", Boston University, June 18-21, 1987. Repr. 1990 in W.R. Connor *et al.*, Aspects of Athenian Democracy (= C&M Dissertationes 11), p. 71-99. [537

Hansen, M.H.: Was Athens a Democracy? Popular rule, liberty and equality in ancient and modern political thought (= HistFilosMed 59). Kbh., 1989. 47 pp. [538

Nielsen, T.H. *et al.*: Athenian Grave Monuments and Social Class. In: GRBS 30, 1989, 411-420. [539

Gabrielsen, V.: Trierarchic Symmories. In: C&M 41, 1990, 89-118. [540

Hansen, M.H. *et al.*: The Demography of the Attic Demes : the evidence of the Sepulchral Inscriptions. In: ARID 19, 1990, 25-44. [541

Hansen, M.H.: Diokles' Law (Dem. 24.42) and the Revision of the Athenian Corpus of Laws in the Archonship of Eukleides. In: C&M 41, 1990, 63-71. [542

Hansen, M.H.: The Political Powers of the People's Court in Fourth-Century Athens. In: The Greek City from Homer to Alexander. Eds. O. Murray & S. Price. Oxford, 1990, 215-243. [543

Hansen, M.H.: Review of Ober, J.: Mass and Elite in Democratic Athens ... Princeton 1989. In: CR 40, 1990, 348-356. [544

Hansen, M.H. & Pedersen, L.: The Size of the Council of the Areopagos and its Social Composition in the Fourth Century B.C . In: C&M 41, 1990, 73-78. [545

Hansen, M.H.: When was Selection by Lot of Magistrates introduced in Athens? In: C&M 41, 1990, 55-61. [546

Hansen, O.: The Date of the Alliance Between Athens and Egesta (Nr 37 M.-L.). In: Hermes 118, 1990, 376-377. [547

Hansen, O.: On the date of the Athenian decree regulating the offering of first-fruits at Eleusis. In: Eirene 27, 1990, 47-48. [548

Gabrielsen, V.: The Athenian trierarchy. Odense, 1991. 504 pp. – Thesis <= DOAII no 556>. [549

Hansen, M.H.: The Athenian democracy in the age of Demosthenes : structure, principles and ideology. Oxford, 1991. 410 pp. [550

Hansen, M.H.: Response to Douglas MacDowell. In: Symposion 1990: Vorträge zur griechischen und hellenistischen Rechtsgeschichte. Ed. M. Gagarin (= AGR 8). Köln, 1991, 199-201. [551

Rubinstein, L. et al.: Adoption in Hellenistic and Roman Athens. In: C&M 42, 1991, 139-151. [552

2. Archaeological subjects

Bundgaard, J.A.: The excavation of the Athenian Acropolis 1882-1890. The original drawings, edited from the papers of Georg Kawerau (= University of Copenhagen. Institute of Classical and Near Eastern Archaeology. Publication 1). Kbh., 1974. 131 pp + 227 pls. [553

See also no 302

Bundgaard, J. A.: Parthenon and the Mycenaean City on the Heights (= Publications of the National Museum. Archaeological-historical series 17). Kbh., 1976. 194 pp. [554

Jeppesen, K.: Where was the So-Called Erechtheion? In: AJA 83, 1979, 381-394. [555

Skovgaard-Hansen, M.: Athéna invisible. Iconologie de l'Acropole. In: Culture, science et développement. Mélanges en l'honneur de Charles Morazé. Toulouse, 1979, 67-87. – Ideological interpretation of the plan of the Acropolis. [556

Hansen, M.H.: The Athenian *Ecclesia* and the Assembly-Place on the Pnyx. In: GRBS 23, 1982, 241-249. – Repr. with addenda in: The Athenian Ecclesia <no 490>, 25-34. [557

Haugsted, I.: The Architect Christian Hansen : Drawings, letters and articles referring to the excavations on the Acropolis 1835-37. In: ARID 10, 1982, 53-96. [558

Jeppesen, K.: Further Inquieries on the Location of the Erechtheion and Its Relationship to the Temple of the Polias. 1: Προστομιαῖον and Προστομίον. In: AJA 87, 1983, 325-333. [559

Jeppesen, K.: Evidence for the Restoration of the East Pediment Reconsidered in the Light of Recent Achievements. In: Parthenon-Kongress: Basel, 4.-8. April 1982. Referate und Berichte. Ed. E. Berger. Mainz, 1984, 267-277; 427-439. [560

Hansen, M.H.: Two Notes on the Pnyx. In: GRBS 26, 1985, 241-250. – Repr. with addenda in: The Athenian Ecclesia 2 <no 530>, 129-141. [561

Hansen, P.A.: The Potter Nicomachus and his Dedication (IG 14.652 = CEG 396). In: ZPE 58, 1985, 231-233. [562

Papanicolaou Christensen, A.: Αθήνα 1818-1853: Έργα Δανων καλλιτεχνων = Athens 1818-1853 : Views of Athens by Danish artists. Athens, 1985. 191 pp. (Partly relevant) [563

Hansen, M.H.: The Construction of Pnyx II and the Introduction of Assembly Pay. In: C&M 37, 1986, 89-98. – Repr. with addenda in: The Athenian Ecclesia 2 <no 530>, 143-153. [564

Jeppesen, K.: The theory of the alternative Erechtheion. Premises, definition, and implications (= Acta Jutlandica 63:1 (= Acta Jutlandica Humanistisk serie 60). Århus, 1987. 112 pp. [565

Jeppesen,K.:Once again: Where was the Erechtheion? In: Πρακτικά του XII Διεθνούς συνεδρίου κλασικής αρχαιαλογίας, Αθήνα Σεπτεμβρίου 1983. Athens, 1988, 77-80 [566

Kiilerich, B.: Bluebeard – A Snake-Tailed Geryon? In: OpAth 17, 1988, 123-136. [567

Kiilerich, B.: The Athenian Acropolis : the position of lions and leopards. In: AArch 59, 1988 [1989], 229-234. [568

Kiilerich, B.: The Olive-tree Pediment and the Daughters of Kekrops. In: ActaAArtHist, Ser. altera in 8vo, 7, 1989, 1-21. [569

Bendtsen, M.: The Acropolis and the Athenian City Plan. In: The Classical Heritage ... <no 1182>, 1990, 209-218. – On sketches by the architect Christian Hansen, some of which are of relevance. [570

BOETHIA
Hansen, O.: Apollo/Artemis at Histiaia/Oreos. In: ZPE 54, 1984, 132. – Comment on F. Cairns in Phoenix 37, 1983, 16-37. [571

Hansen, O.: Hestia Boulaia at Erythrai. In: AC 54, 1985, 274-276. [572

Hansen, O.: On the archaic constitution of Erythrae. In: AC 55, 1986, 323. [573

CRETE
Hallager, E.: Final Palatial Crete : An Essay in Minoan Chronology. In: Studies ... <no 1181>, 1988, 11-21. [574

Cnossus
Hallager, E.: The Mycenaean Palace at Knossos. Evidence for Final Destruction in the III B Period (= Medelhavsmuseet. Memoir 1). Stockholm, 1977. 120 pp. [575

Hallager, E.: The History of the Palace of Knossos in the Late Minoan Period. In: SMEA 19, 1978, 17-33. [576

Hallager, E.: A "Harvest Festival Room" in the Minoan Palaces? An Architectural Study of the Pillar Crypt Area at Knossos. In: The Function of the Minoan Palaces. Proceed. IV Intern. Symposium at the Swedish Institute in Athens (= SkrAth 35) Stockholm, 1987, 169-171. [577

Kydonia
Hallager, E.: Minoan Kydonia. Excavations 1973. In: AAA 6, 1973, 439-448. [578

Hallager, E. & Styrenius, C.-G.: De svensk-grekiska ütgrävningarna i Chania. In: Hellenika 1, 1977, 6. [579

Hallager, E. & Tzedakis, Y.: The Greek-Swedish Excavations at Kastelli Chania 1976 and 1977. In: AAA 11, 1978, 31-46. [580

Hallager, E. & Styrenius, C.-G.: De svensk-grekiska ütgrävningarna i Chania på västra Kreta. In: Hellenika 18, 1981, 9-11. [581

Hallager, E. & Tzedakis, Y.: The Greek-Swedish Excavations Castelli, Khania (1978 and 1979). In: AAA 15, 1982, 21-30. [582

Hallager, B.P.: Italians in Late Bronze Age Khania. In: Magna Grecia e Mondo Miceneo. Atti XXII Convegno di Studi sulla Magna Grecia, Taranto 7-11 ottobre 1982. Taranto, 1983, 358-363 . [583

Hallager, B.P.: A New Social Class in Late Bronze Age Crete: Foreign Traders in Khania. In: Minoan Society. Proceed. of the Cambridge Colloquium 1981. Eds. O. Krzyszkowska & L. Nixon. Bristol, 1983, 111-119. – On hand-made pottery in South Italian ceramic tradition. [584

Hallager, E. & Tzedakis, Y.: The Greek-Swedish Excavations at Kastelli, Khania 1980. In: AAA 16, 1983, 3-17. [585

Hallager, E. & Tzedakis, Y.: The Greek-Swedish Excavations at Kastelli, Khania 1982-83. In: AAA 17, 1984, 3-20. [586

Hallager, B.P.: Crete and Italy in the Late Bronze Age III Period. In: AJA 89, 1985, 293-305. [587

Hallager, E. & Tzedakis, Y.: The Greek-Swedish Excavations at Kastelli, Khania 1984. In: AAA 18, 1985, 9-28. [588

Hallager, E. & Tzedakis, Y.: The Greek-Swedish Excavations at Kastelli, Khania 1987. In: AAA 19, 1986, 11-26. [589

Hallager, E.: The Greek-Swedish Excavations at Khania. In: Proceed. V Intern. Cretological Congr. at Ag. Nikolaous 25. Sept. – 1st Oct. 1981. Heraklion, 1986, 139-154. [590

Hallager, B.P.: Some LM IIIB:1 Floor Deposits at Khania, West Crete (Summary). In: Kolloquium zur Ägäischen Vorgeschichte, Mannheim 20-22.2 1986 (= Schriften des Deutschen Archäologien-Verbandes 9) 1987, 89. [591

Hallager, E.: The Late Minoan IIIA:2 and IIIB Periods in Khania (A Summary). In: Kolloquium zur Ägäischen Vorgeschichte <cf. no 592>, 1987, 88. [592

Hallager, E. & Tzedakis, Y.: The Greek-Swedish Excavations at Kastelli, Khania : I The 1989 excavation ; II The 1990 excavation. In: AAA 21, 1988, 15-55. [593

Hallager, E.: Khania and Crete ca. 1375-1200 B.C . In: CretSt 1, 1988, 115-124, Pls 62-71. [594

Tzedakis, Y.; Hallager, E.; Andreanaki-Vlasaki, M.: Προϊστορικές και κλασικές αρχαίοθητες. Πόλη Χανίον. In: Κρητικη Έστία 2, 1988, 275-277. [595

Hallager, E. & Vlasakis, M.: Khania. In: EAA, supplementary volume 2. Roma, 1989, 112-115. [596

Hallager, B.P.: LM II and Khania. In: Acts VI Intern. Cretological Congr., Khania, 24-30 august 1986. Vol. A2. Khania, 1990, 77-84. [597

Mallia
Pelon, O.; Andersen, E.; Olivier, J.P.: Le palais de Mallia, 5 (= Études crétoises 25). Paris, 1980. xii + 264 pp. [598

ELIS

Hansen, O.: On the Helmets Dedicated by Hieron to Zeus at Olympia. In: Hermes 118, 1990, 498. [599

See also no 316

EUBOEA
Mørkholm, O.: Review of Picard, O.: Chalcis et la confédération eubéenne. Étude de numismatique et d'histoire. Paris 1979. In: Gnomon 52, 1980, 451-456. [600

HALONESSOS
Hansen, O.: On the Site of Nea. In: Eranos 87, 1989, 70-72. – On IG II2 334 + SEG 18,13; identification as Agios Efestatios suggested. [601

LACONIA
Poulsen, B.: A Relief from Croceae : Dioscuri in Roman Laconia. In: Recent Danish Research ... <no 793>, 1991, 235-248. – Includes (pp. 235-241) an excursus by J. Carlsen: The Inscription CIL III 493 and the Administration of the Quarry at Croceae. [602

PHOCIS
Poulsen, F.: Delphi. Washington, D.C., 1973. xi + 338 pp. (Reprint of the edition London 1920 <PAH no 2060>). – Translation of Oraklet i Delphi. Kbh., 1919. [603

Hansen, E.: Emplois de pierres brutes dans les constructions, surtout à Delphes. In: Mélanges helléniques offerts à George Daux. Paris, 1974, 159-179. [604

Algreen-Ussing, G. & Bramsnæs A.: Fouilles de Delphes II : Topographie et architecture. Le sanctuaire d'Apollon. Atlas. Paris, 1975. iii + 75 pls. [605

Daux, G. & Hansen, E.: Fouilles de Delphes. Tome 2: Topographie et architecture. Le trésor de Siphnos. Paris, 1987. 253 pp, 108 pls. [606

Hansen, O.: *Epigraphia Belliaca*. On the Dedication of the Athenian Portico at Delphi. In: C&M 40, 1989, 133-134. [607

Hansen, E.: Versetzen von Baugliedern am griechischen Tempel. In: Bautechnik der Antike. Intern. Kolloquium in Berlin vom 15.-17. Februar 1990. Ed. A. Hoffmann. Mainz, 1991, 72-79. – The examples are drawn from Delphi. [608

RHODES

Dietz, S.: Excavations and surveys in Southern Rhodes : the Mycenaean period (= Nationalmuseets skrifter 22:1 (= Lindos 4:1. Results of the Carlsberg Foundation excavations in Rhodes 1902-1914)). Kbh., 1984. 120 pp. [609

Melander, T.: Vroulia: Town Plan and Gate. In: Archaeology in the Dodecanese <no 443>, 1988, 83-87. [610

THERA

Friedrich, W.L.; Friborg, R.; Tauber, H.: Two Radiocarbon Dates of the Minoan eruption on Santorini (Greece). In: Thera and the Aegean World II. Papers and proceedings of the second intern. Scientific congr., Santorini, Greece, August 1978. London, 1980, 241-243. [610a

Hansen, O.: Were the native inhabitants of Thera called helots by the Spartan colonists? In: AJPh 105, 1984, 326-327. [611

Hammer, C.U. *et al.*: The Minoan Eruption of Santorini in Greece dated to 1645 BC? In: Nature 328, 1987, 517-519. – Cf. also Hammer, C.U. *et al.*: The Dating of the Santorini eruption – a reply, in: Nature 332, 1988, 401. [612

Friedrich, W.L; Wagner, P.; Tauber, H.: Radiocarbon dated plant remains from the Akrotiri excavation on Santorini, Greece. In: Thera and the Aegaean World III. Proceedings of the Third intern. Scientific congr., Santorini, Greece, 3-9 September 1989, Vol. 3. London, 1990, 188-196. [612a

THRACE

Hansen, O.: On the site of Brea. In: OpAth 15, 1984, 187. [613

ITALY AND SICILY

Carlsen, J.: Lo sviluppo urbano nelle *regiones* II e III del principato. Edilizia pubblica ed evoluzione dell'agricoltura. In: Studies ... <no 1181>, 1988, 139-147. [614

Strøm, I.: Relations between Etruria and Campania around 700 B.C. In: Greek Colonists and native populations. Proceed. of the first Australian Congr. of Classical Archaeology held in honour of Emeritus Professor A.D.Trendall. Oxford, 1990, 87-97. [615

CAMPANIA
Skydsgaard, J.E.: Review of D'Arms, J.H.: Romans on the Bay of Naples ... Cambridge, Mass. 1970. In: JRS 61, 1971, 277-278. [616

Dybkjær Larsen, J.: The Water Towers in Pompeii. In: ARID 11, 1982, 41-67. [617

Skydsgaard, J.E.: Pompeji : en romersk landsortsstad. Göteborg, 1982. 187 pp. – Translation of Pompeii. Kbh., 1970 <DOAI no 782>. [618

Neiiendam, K.: Theatrical Murals at the House of Publius Casca Longus. In: ARID 12, 1983, 72-79. [619

Andersen, F.G.: Pompeian painting. Some practical aspects of creation. In: ARID 14, 1985, 113-128. [620

Neiiendam, K.: A Fresco showing a Hellenistic Performance of Euripides' "Iphigenia in Aulis". In: ARID 16, 1987, 53-59. [621

Mouritsen, H.: Elections, Magistrates and Municipal Élite : Studies in Pompeian Epigraphy (= ARID Supplementum 15). Roma, 1988. 224 pp. [622

Mouritsen, H.: A Note on Pompeian Epigraphy and Social Structure. In: C&M 41, 1990, 131-149. [623

Gradel, I. & Mouritsen, H.: Nero in Pompeian Politics. Edicta Munerum and Imperial Flaminates in Late Pompeii. In: ZPE 87, 1991, 145-155. – On CIL IV 1185, 3884, 7992, 7995. [624

Horsnæs, H.W.: The Ager Picentinus. In: Recent Danish Research ... <no 793>, 1991, 219-234. [625

ETRURIA
Poulsen, M.; Saxtorph, N.M.; Skydsgaard, J.E.: Ancient and modern Road-Systems near Tuscania : Continuity or Discontinuity. In: ARID 8, 1977, 19-38. [626

Poulsgaard Markussen, E.: Painted tombs in Etruria : a bibliography (= Skrifter udgivet af Institut for klassiske studier). Odense, 1979. 253 pp. – Repr. with corrections and additions 1981 and 1983. [627

Rathje, A.: Die Phönizier in Etrurien. In: Die Phönizier im Zeitalter Homers. Eds. U. Gehring & H.G. Niemeyer. Mainz, 1990, 33-44. [628

Strøm, I.: Il ruolo del commercio fenicio del Villanoviano in Etruria. Un'ipotesi. In: Atti II Congr. Intern. di Studi Fenici e Punici <cf. no 415>, 1991, 323-331. [629

Cosa
Carlsen, J.: Considerations on Cosa and Ager Cosanus. In: ARID 13, 1984, 49-58. [630

Monte Becco
Strøm, I.: [Monte Becco]. In: AR 1979-1980, 64. [631

Poggio Civitate
Andersen, H.D.: The feline waterspouts of the lateral sima from the Upper Building at Poggio Civitate, Murlo. In: OpRom 18, 1990, 61-98. [632

San Giovenale
Helbæk, H.: Appendix [Examination of seeds]. In: San Giovenale, vol. II,2: Excavations in Area B, 1957-1960. By E. Berggren and K. Berggren (= Skr-Rom 26, 2.2). Stockholm, 1981, 57. [633

Malcus, B.: Area D (ovest). In: San Giovenale. Materiali e problemi. Atti del Simposio all'Istituto Svedese di Studi Classici a Roma, 6 aprile 1983. Eds. S. Forsberg and B.E. Thomasson (= SkrRom 41). Stockholm, 1984, 37-60. [634

Satricum
Ginge, B.: Selected Sporadic Finds from Satricum. In: MededRom 47, 1987, 17-33. [635

Ginge, B.: Satricum (Latina) : Sporadic Finds from the Excavations 1977-1980. In: NSc 1984-1985 [1988], 221-251. [636

Ginge, B.: Review of Knoop, R.R.: Antefixa satricana ... Assen 1987. In: AJA 93, 1989, 614-615. [637

Ginge, B.: Review of Maaskant-Kleibrink, M.: Settlement excavations at Borgo Le Ferriere (Satricum), 1 ... Groningen 1987. In: AJA 93, 1989, 151-152. [638

Tarquinia
Poulsgaard Markussen, E.: Tomba del Gorgoneion reviewed (= Skrifter udgivet af Institut for klassiske studier). Odense, 1982. 16 pp. – Revised version (title unchanged) published in ARID 12, 1983, 55-63. [639

Poulsgaard Markussen, E.: Out of Tarquinia : The Grotta Penta at Blera. In: ARID 14, 1985, 17-36. [640

Poulsgaard Markussen, E.: Out of Tarquinia : A Note on Another Painted Tomb at Blera. In: Recent Danish Research ... <no 793>, 1991, 73-81. – The tomb (here named Tomba Dipinta) is closely related to the Grotta Penta. [641

Volterra
Nielsen, M.: The Relationships between Volterra and Its Territory Illustrated by Urns from the Hellenistic Period. In: Die Welt der Etrusker : Intern. Kolloquium Berlin 1988. Eds. H. Heres & M. Kunze. Berlin, 1990, 201-217. [642

LATIUM (OUTSIDE ROME)
Fischer-Hansen, T.: Fortificazioni nel Lazio e a Ficana nell'età di ferro. In: Ficana <no 652>, 1981, 59-65. [643

Licht, K.d.F.: Cisterna presso la via di Poli. In: ARID 13, 1984, 87-90. – The cistern is dated to the 1st cent. AD. [644

Antrum Albanum

Licht, K.d.F.: Antrum Albanum : Report on a measurement survey conducted at Ninfeo Bergantino near Castel Gandolfo. In: ARID 7, 1974, 37-66. [645

Ficana

Bartolini, G.; Fischer-Hansen, T.; Zevi, F.: Ficana. In: StEtr 45, 1977, 432-434. [646

Ficana : rassegne preliminare delle campagne archeologiche 1975-1977 [Prefazione par V.S.M. Scrinari e S. Skovgaard Jensen] (= Itinerari Ostiensi 2). Roma, 1977. 48 pp, 31 pls. – Contains unsigned articles by members of the Scandinavian institutes in Rome (including Accademia di Danimarca) and the staff of Soprintendenza archeologica di Ostia. Published for an exhibition in Ostia Antica, november 1977. [647

Zevi, F. et al.: Saggi di scavo sul sito dell'antica Ficana. In: PP 32, 1977, 330-339. [648

Fischer-Hansen, T. et al.: Ficana. In: QArchEtr 1 (= ArchLaz 1), 1978, 35-41. [649

Fischer-Hansen, T.: The Italo-Nordic excavations at Ficana. Some aspects of the proto-history of Lazio. In: Greece and Italy in the Classical World. Acta XI Intern. Congr. of Classical Archaeology London 3-9 september 1978. Eds. J.N. Coldstream & M.A.R. Colledge. London, 1979, 189. – Summary of paper. [650

Rathje, A.: Ficana: lo scavo di una città protostorica alle foci del Tevere. In: Mondo Archeologico 48, 1980, 10-13. [651

Ficana. Una pietra miliare sulla strada per Roma. Mostra itinerante degli scavi italo-nordici a Ficana (Acilia) (1975-1980). Eds. R. Brandt & A. Rathje. Roma, 1981. 160 pp, 52 pls. – Italian version of Ficana. En milesten på veien til Roma : en vandreudstilling om de felles italiensk-nordiske utgravningar (1975-80) utenfor Roma ... Kbh., 1980 <DOAII no 766>. [652

Fischer-Hansen, T. & Pavolini, C.: Ficana: introduzione agli scavi. In: Ficana <no 562>, 1981, 38-51. [653

Nielsen, I. & Pietillä-Castrén, L.: Ficana nella tarda età republicana e nella prima etá imperiale. In: Ficana <no 562>, 1981, 108-110. [654

Rathje, A.: Il processo di urbanizzazione nel Lazio e a Roma fino al VII secolo a.C. In: Ficana <no 562>, 1981, 22-30. [655

Algreen-Ussing, G. & Fischer-Hansen, T.: Ficana, le saline e le vie della regione bassa del Tevere. In: QArchEtr 11 (= ArchLaz 7), 1985, 65-71. [656

Fischer-Hansen, T.: Scavi di Ficana. Vol. 1: Topografia generale. Con la collaborazione di Gregers Algreen-Ussing e con un contributo di Carlo Pavolini. Roma, 1990. 152 pp, 6 pls. [657

La Giostra
Moltesen, M.: La Giostra – Tellenae? In: QArchEtr 1 (= ArchLaz 1), 1978, 60-63. [658

Moltesen, M.: La Giostra (Roma). Rapporto preliminare sullo scavo di sondaggio del novembre 1976. In: NSc 1980 [1981], 51-58. [659

Moltesen, M.: Località La Giostra. In: BullCom 92, 1987-1988, 559-566. [660

Ostia
Schiøler, T.: An attempt to locate lead pipes in Ostia Antica. In: Prospezioni Archeologiche 6, 1971, 93-94. – Name given as Schioler. [661

Nielsen, I. & Schiøler, T.: The Water System in the Baths of Mithras in Ostia. In: ARID 9, 1980, 149-159. [662

Tibur
Hannestad, N.: Über das Grabmal des Antinoos : Topographische und thematische Studien im Canopus-Gebiet der Villa Adriana. In: ARID 11, 1982, 69-108. [663

Lund, H.: Eine Vermessung des 18. Jahrhunderts der Villa Adriana. In: ARID 10, 1982, 41-52. – Survey ascribed to the architect C.F. Harsdorff. [664

ROME

Licht, K.d.F.: Untersuchungen an den Trajansthermen zu Rom (= ARID Supplementum 7). Kbh., 1974. 48 pp. [665

Licht, K.d.F.: Marginalia on Trajan's Baths in Rome. In: Studia Romana ... <no 1177>, 1976, 87-95. [666

Meyer, J.C.: Roman History in Light of the Import of Attic Vases to Rome and Etruria in the 6th and 5th Centuries B.C. In: ARID 9, 1980, 47-68. [667

Città e architettura nella Roma imperiale. Atti del seminario del 27 ottobre 1981 nel 25 anniversario dell'Accademia di Danimarca. Ed. Kjeld de Fine Licht (= ARID Supplementum 10). Odense, 1983. 233 pp. [668

Licht, K.d.F.: Scavi alle Sette Sale. In: Città e architettura ... <no 668>, 1983, 186-202. [669

Meyer, J.C.: Pre-Republican Rome : An Analysis of the Cultural and Chronological Relations 1000-500 BC (= ARID Supplementum 11). Odense, 1983. 210 pp, 2 pls. – Thesis. [670

Schiøler, T. & Wikander, Ö.: A Roman Water-mill in the Baths of Caracalla. In: OpRom 14, 1983, 47-64. [671

Kjærgaard, J.: From "Memoria Apostolorum" to Basilica Apostolorum: On the Early Christian Cult-centre on the Via Appia. In: ARID 13, 1984, 59-76. [672

Schiøler, T.: A Vitruvian Mill in Rome = Un Moulin Vitruvien à Rome. In: The International Molinological Society. Transactions of the Fifth Symposium, France 1982, April 5-10. Paris, 1984, 428-438. [673

Licht, K.d.F. et al.: Colle Oppio. In: Roma. Arceologia nel centro, 2. Roma, 1985, 467-477. [674

Nylander, C. & Zahle, J.: Indagini al Tempio dei Castori. In: QArchEtr 11 (= ArchLaz 7), 1985, 135-138. [675

Guldager, P. & Slej, K.: Gli scavi scandinavi nel Foro Romano. Il tempio di Castore e Polluce. In: ArchViva 5.4, 1986, 24-37. [676

Nielsen, I. & Zahle, J.: The temple of Castor and Pollux on the Forum Romanum : a preliminary report on the Scandinavian excavations 1983-1985 (I). In: AArch 56, 1985 [1987], 1-29. [677

Nielsen, I. & Grønne, C.: Ultime indagini al Tempio dei Castori. In: QArchEtr 14 (= ArchLaz 8), 1987, 83-87. [678

Licht, K.d.F.: Review of Rasch, J.J.: Das Maxentius-Mausoleum an der Via Appia in Rom. Mainz 1984. In: Gnomon 60, 1988, 569-571. [679

Nedergaard, E.: Nuove indagini sull'arco di Augusto nel Foro Romano 1985-1987. In: QArchEtr 16 (= ArchLaz 9), 1988, 37-43. [680

Nedergaard, E.: Zur Problematik der Augustusbögen auf den Forum Romanum. In: Kaiser Augustus und die verlorene Republik. Mainz, 1988, 224-237. [681

Poulsen, B. & Grønne, C.: Ricerce nel Vicus Tuscus lungo il lato ovest del tempio dei Castori. In: QArchEtr 16 (= ArchLaz 9), 1988, 27-31. – Includes pp. 30-31 appendix by C. Grønne: Terrecotte architettoniche dal Vicus Tuscus. [682

Sande, S. & Zahle, J.: Der Tempel der Dioskuren auf den Forum Romanum. In: Kaiser Augustus und die verlorene Republik <cf. no 681>, 1988, 213-219. [683

Ginge, B.; Becker, M.; Guldager, P.: Of Roman extraction. In: Archaeology 42, 1989, 34-37. – On dental bridgework, found near the Temple of Castor and Pollux. [684

Hansen, J.: Untersuchungen an Bleiwasserrohren für die Trajansthermen zu Rom. In: MittLeichtweiss 103, 1989, 105-119. [685

Nielsen, I.: The temple of Castor and Pollux on the Forum Romanum : a preliminary report on the Scandinavian excavations 1983-1987 (II). In: AArch 59, 1988 [1989], 1-14. [686

Grønne, C.: Fragments of Architectural Terracottas from the First Temple of Castor and Pollux on the Forum Romanum : a preliminary report. In: ARID 19, 1990, 105-117. [687

Licht, K.d.F.: Untersuchungen an den Trajansthermen zu Rom 2: Sette Sale. Mit Beiträgen von J. Lund und J. Hansen (= ARID Supplementum 19). Romae, 1990. 125 pp. – Appendices by J. Lund: Lampen aus Terrakotta (pp. 105-110), and by J. Hansen: Wasserleitungen aus Bleirohren (pp. 111-125). [688

Nielsen, I.: The Forum paving and the Temple of Castor and Pollux. In: ARID 19, 1990, 89-104. [689

Nielsen, I.: Review of Broise, H. *et al.*: Le balneum des Frères Arvales ... Roma 1987. In: BJb 190, 1990, 685-687. [690

Hertz, L.E.: Roma : aspetti della fortificazione fluviale. In: Recent Danish Research ... <no 793>, 1991, 297-310. [691

SICILY

Fischer-Hansen, T.: Sizilien und Dänemark. In: The Classical Heritage ... <no 1182>, 1990, 169-188. – On architectural drawings by Simon Christian Pontoppidan 1821/22, of which some are of relevance. [692

UMBRIA

Lavrsen, J.: Montefortino. In: NotMilano 27-28, 1981, 5-26. [693

EUROPE OUTSIDE GREECE AND ITALY

Bekker-Nielsen, T.: The geography of power. Studies in the urbanization of Roman North-West Europe (= BAR International Series 477). Oxford, 1989. 135 pp. [694

Ørsted, P.: Ad Publicanos. Zwei Zollstationen und ihre Bedeutung für die Territorialgeschichte von Vienna bzw. Emona. In: ActaArchHung 41, 1989, 175-188. [695

BRITANNIA
Østergaard, J.S.: Review of Cunliffe, B.: Fishbourne. A Roman palace ... Baltimore 1971. In: IJNA 1, 1972, 239. [696

GALLIA
Cochet, A. & Hansen, J.: Conduites et objets de plomb gallo-romains de Vienne (Isère) (= Gallia Supplement 46). Paris, 1986. 229 pp. [697

Bekker-Nielsen, T.: Rivers and urban development in Roman Gaul. In: Montagnes, fleuves, forêts dans l'histoire. Barrières ou lignes de convergence? Travaux présentés au XVIe Congr. intern. des sciences historiques, Stuttgart, août 1985. Ed. J.-F. Bergier. St. Katarinen, 1989, 111-122. [698

GERMANIA
Andersen, F.G.: Eine römische Wanddekoration aus Mainz. In: MZ 73/74, 1978/79, 293-299, Pls 56-57. [699

NORICUM
Harding, M. & Jacobsen, G.: Die Bedeutung der zivilen Zuwanderung aus Norditalien für die Entwicklung der Städte in Noricum und Pannonia. In: C&M 39, 1988, 117-206. [700

Harding, M. & Jacobsen, G.: Norditalienische Zuwanderung nach Celia während der ersten zwei Jahrhunderte n. Chr. In: ActaArchHung 41, 1989, 227-232. [701

ASIA MINOR

Isager, S.: Kings and Gods in the Seleucid Empire. A Question of Landed Property in Asia Minor. In: Religion ... <no 1099>, 1990, 79-90. [702

CARIA
Pedersen, P.: Some general trends in the architectural lay-out in 4th century B.C. Caria. In: Architecture and Society in Hecatomnid Caria. Eds. P.T. Linder & P. Hellström (= Boreas 17). Uppsala, 1989, 9-14. [703

Zahle, J.: Review of Roos, P.: Survey of rock-cut chamber tombs in Caria I ... Göteborg 1985, and of Pekridou, A.: Das Alketas-Grab in Termessos, Tübingen 1986. In: JHS 110, 1990, 262-263. [704

Halicarnassus

Jeppesen, K. & Zahle, J.: The Site of the Mausoleum at Halicarnassus Reexcavated. In: AJA 77, 1973, 336-338. [705

Jeppesen, K.: Nisi absoluto iam. Observations on the buildings of the Mausoleum at Halikarnassus. In: Türk Tarih Kurumu ... Mélanges Mansel, vol. 2. Ankara, 1974, 735-748. [706

Jeppesen, K. & Zahle, J.: Investigations on the Site of the Mausoleum 1970/1973. In: AJA 79, 1975, 67-79. [707

Jeppesen, K.: Neue Ergebnisse zur Wiederherstellung des Mausolleions von Halikarnassos (4. Vorläufiger Bericht der dänischen Halikarnassosexpedition). In: IstMitt 26, 1976, 47-99. [708

Jeppesen, K.: Zur Gründung und Baugeschichte des Mausolleions von Halikarnassos. In: IstMitt 27/28, 1977/78, 169-211. [709

Jeppesen, K.: The Reconstruction of the Mausoleum. In: Proceed. X Intern. Congr. of Classical Archaeology, Ankara-Izmir 1973. Ankara, 1978, 535-542. [710

Zahle, J.: The Mausoleum-Site before the Mausoleum. In: Proceed. X Intern. Congr. of Classical Archaeology <cf. no 710>, 1978, 529-534. [711

Jeppesen, K.: The Mausoleum at Halicarnassus. In: Greece and Italy in the Classical World <cf. no 650>, 1979, 232. – Summary of paper. [712

Højlund, F. & Aaris-Sørensen, K.: The Maussolleion at Halikarnassos : Reports of the Danish Archaeological Expeditions to Bodrum. Vol. 1 : The Sacrificial Deposit. [Introduction by K. Jeppesen]. (= Jysk Arkæologisk Selskabs skrifter 15:1). Århus, 1981. 110 pp. [713

Højlund, F.: The Maussolleion sacrifice. In: AJA 87, 1983, 145-152. [714

Jeppesen, K.: Zu den Proportionen des Maussolleions von Halikarnass. In: Bauplanung und Bautheorie der Antike (= Diskussionen zur Archäologischen Bauforschung 4). Berlin, 1983, 167-174. [715

Pedersen, P.: Zwei ornamentierte Säulenhalse aus Halikarnassos. In: JdI 98, 1983, 87-121. [716

Jeppesen, K. & Luttrell, A.: The Maussolleion at Halikarnassos. Reports of the Danish Archaeological Expedition to Bodrum, Vol. 2 : The Written Sources and Their Archaeological Background (= Jysk Arkæologisk Selskabs skrifter 15:2). Århus, 1986. 224 pp. [717

Pedersen, P.: The Maussolleion-Terrace at Halicarnassus and 4th c. B.C. Planning in South-Western Asia Minor. In: Πρακρικά του XII Διθνούς συνεδρίου κλασικής αρχαιαλογίας, <cf. no 566>, 1988, 155-159. [718

Pedersen, P.: Town-planning in Halicarnassus and Rhodes. In: Archaeology in the Dodecanese <no 443>, 1988, 98-103. [719

Pedersen, P.: Two Ionic Buildings in Halicarnassus. In: V Araştirma Sonuçlari Toplantisi, 1988. Ankara, 1988, 359-368. [720

Jeppesen, K.: What did the Maussolleion look like? In: Architecture and Society in Hecatomnid Caria <cf. no 703>, 1989, 15-22. [721

Pedersen, P.: Restivity measurings and magnetometer measurings in ancient Halikarnassos 1988. In: V Arkeometri Sonuçlari Toplantisi, 1989. Ankara, 1990, 41-51. [722

Pedersen, P.: The Maussolleion at Halikarnassos. Reports of the Danish Archaeological Expeditions to Bodrum, Vol. 3: The Maussolleion Terrace and Accessory Structures. 1-2 (= Jysk Arkæologisk Selskabs skrifter 15:3,1-2). Højbjerg, 1991. 208, 134 pp. – Thesis <= DOAII no 778>. [723

LYCIA
Kjeldsen, K. & Zahle, J.: Lykische Gräber, Ein vorläufiger Bericht. In: AA 1975, 312-350. [724

Hansen, E. & Le Roy, C.: Le Létôon de Xanthos : les deux temples de Léto. In: RA 1976, 317-336. [725

Zahle, J.: Archaic Tumulus Tombs in Central Lycia (Phellos). In: AArch 46, 1975 [1976], 77-94. [726

Kjeldsen, K. & Zahle, J.: A Dynastic Tomb in Central Lycia : New Evidence for the Study of Lycian Architecture and History in the Classical Period. In: AArch 47, 1976 [1977], 29-46. [727

Zahle, J.: Review of Demargne, P.: Fouilles de Xanthos, 5: Tombes-maisons ... Paris 1974. In: Gnomon 49, 1977, 404-411. [728

Zahle, J.: Lykische Felsgräber mit Reliefs aus dem 4. Jahrhunderts v.Chr. : Neue und alte Funde. In: JdI 94, 1979, 245-346. [729

Zahle, J.: Lycian Tombs and Lycian Cities. In: Actes du colloque sur la Lycie antique, Bibliothèque de l'Institut français d'études anatoliennes d'Istanbul 27, 1980, 37-49. [730

Zahle, J.: Arkæologiske studier i lykiske klippegrave. Kbh., 1983. ix + 174 pp. – Summary in German p. 160-166. – Thesis <= DOAII no 806>. [731

Hansen, E.: Le temple de Létô au Létôon de Xanthos. In: RA 1991, 323-340. [732

Zahle, J.: Achaemenid influence in Lycia (coinage, scupture, architecture). Evidence for political changes during the 5th century B.C. In: Achaemenid history 6. Leiden, 1991, 145-160. (Partly relevant) [733

CYPRUS, SYRIA AND PALESTINE

CYPRUS

Sørensen, L.W.: Canadian Palaepaphos Survey Project : Preliminary Report of the 1980 Ceramic Finds. In: RDAC 1983, 283-299. – Survey at present-day Kouklia. [734

Rupp, D.W. *et al.*: Canadian Palaepaphos (Cyprus) Survey Project : Second Preliminary Report, 1980-1982. In: JFA 11, 1984, 133-154. [735

Rupp, D.W. *et al.*: The Canadian Palaepaphos (Cyprus) Survey Project : Third Preliminary Report, 1983-1985. In: AArch 57, 1986 [1987], 27-45. [736

Sørensen, L.W. *et al.*: Canadian Palaepaphos Survey Project: Second Preliminary Report of the Ceramic Finds 1982-1983. In: RDAC 1987, 259-278. [737

Bekker-Nielsen, T.; Hannestad, N.; Jensen, M.: An Ancient Road on the West Coast of Cyprus. In: RDAC 1991, 203-210. [738

Fejfer, J. & Mathiesen, H.E.: The Danish Akamas-Project. In: RDAC 1991, 211-223. [739

Fejfer, J.; Hannestad, N.; Mathiesen, H.E.: The Danish Archaeological Excavations at Ayios Kononas, Cyprus : A Preliminary Report of the First Season of Work (1989). In: Recent Danish Research ... <no 793>, 1991, 97-109. [740

Fejfer, J. & Mathiesen, H.E.: Excavations at Ayios Kononas uncover Fourth Century C.E. Farm House. In: BiblArch 54,1, 1991, 53-54. [741

SYRIA AND PALESTINE
Riis, P.J.: The Mycenaean expansion in the light of the Danish excavations at Hama and Sukas. In: Acts of the intern. archaeol. Symposium "The Mycenaeans in the Eastern Mediterranean" Nicosia March-April 1972. Nicosia, 1973, 198-206. [742

Riis, P.J.: Griechen in Phönizien. In: MBeitr 8, 1982, 243-260. [743

Lund, J.: Review of Stucky, R.A.: Ras Shamra. Leukos Limen ... Paris 1983. In: BibO 43, 1986, 485-488. (Partly relevant) [744

Ploug, G.: East Syrian Art of 1st Century B.C.-2nd Century A.D. In: East and West <no 1180>, 1988, 129-139. – Identifies Greek, as well as Achamaenid and Western semitic elements. [745

Riis, P.J.: Quelques problèmes de la topographie phénicienne. Usnu, Paltos, Pelléta et les ports de la région. In: Géographique historique au Proche-Orient. Syrie, Phénicie, Arabie, grecques, romaines, byzantines. Actes de la Table ronde, Valbonne 16-18 septembre 1985. Paris, 1988, 315-324. [746

Lund, J.: The Northern Coastline of Syria in the Persian Period – A Survey of the Archaeological Evidence. In: Transeuphratène 2, 1990, 13-36. (Partly relevant) [747

Riis, P.J.: Les problèmes actuels de l'établissement de Grecs sur la côte phénicienne (lieux, dates, modalités). In: Atti II Congr. Intern. di Studi Fenici e Punici <cf. no 415>, 1991, 203-211. [748

Bosra
Finsen, H.: Le levé du théatre romain a Bosra, Syrie. Avec Supplément historique et apercu des travaux de dégagement par S. Mougdad (= ARID Supplementum 6). Kbh., 1972. 24 pp, 19 pls. – Translation of Opmålingen af det romerske teater i Bosra, Syrien. Kbh., 1972 <DOAI no 748>. [749

Caesarea Maritima
Schiøler, T.: The Watermills at the Crocodile River. A turbine mill dated to 345-380 A.D. In: PEQ 121, 1989, 133-143. [750

Gadara
Holm-Nielsen, S.; Nielsen, I.; Andersen, F.G.: The Excavation of Byzantine Baths in Umm Qeis. In: ADAJ 30, 1986, 219-232. (Partly relevant; the building and the finds continue into the post-classical period) [751

Hama
Papanicolaou Christensen, A. & Friis Johansen, C.: Hama. Fouilles et recherches 1931-1938. III:2. Les poteries hellénistiques et les terres sigillées orientales (= Nationalmuseets skrifter. Større beretninger 8). Kbh., 1971 [1972], xii + 208 pp. [752

Ploug, G.: Hama: fouilles et recherches 1931-1938. III:1. The Graeco-Roman town (= Nationalmuseets skrifter. Større beretninger 9). Kbh., 1985. 253 pp, 7 pls. – With an appendix by Adam Bülow-Jacobsen: Gold Amulet, pp. 250-251. [753

Papanicolaou Christensen, A.; Thomsen, R.; Ploug, G.: Hama: fouilles et recherches 1931-1938; III:3. The Graeco-Roman objects of clay, the coins and the necropolis (= Nationalmuseets skrifter. Større beretninger 10). Kbh., 1986. 113 pp. [754

Riis, P.J. et al.: Hama : Fouilles et recherches 1931-1938; II: 2. Les objects de la période dite syro-hittite (Âge du fer). Kbh., 1990. 324 pp. (Of relevance is the section p. 184-189 on Greek imported pottery (catalogue nos. 665-673)) [755

Palmyra
Ploug, G.: A Dated Palmyrene Bust in the Danish National Museum. In: Recent Danish Research ... <no 793>, 1991, 365-378. – On inv. 14489 (bust of Zabad'atê, AD 160). Includes (pp. 376-378) a contribution by F.O. Hvidberg-Hansen: The Inscription on the Palmyrene Bust. [756

Silo
Andersen, F.G.: Shiloh : the Danish Excavations at Tall Sailūn, Palestine in 1926, 1929, 1932 and 1963. Vol. 2: The Remains from the Hellenistic to the Mamlūk Periods (= Publications of the National Museum. Archaeological-historical series 23). Kbh., 1985. 111 pp, 32 pls. (Partly relevant) [757

Sukas
Ploug, G.: Sukas II : The Aegean, Corinthian and Eastern Greek Pottery and Terracottas (= HistFilosSkr 6:2 (= Publications of the Carlsberg Expedition to Phoenicia 2)). Kbh., 1973. 124 pp 20 pls. [758

Riis, P.J.: Tell Sukas. In: The Princeton Encyclopedia of Classical Sites. Princeton, 1976, 891-892. (Partly relevant) [759

Riis, P.J.: Sukas VI : The Graeco-Phoenician Cemetary and Sanctuary at the Southern Harbour (= HistFilosSkr 10:2 (= Publications of the Carlsberg Expedition to Phoenicia 7)). Kbh., 1978. 68 pp. [760

Riis, P.J.: La ville phénicienne de Soukas de la fin de l'âge du bronze à la conquête romaine. In: Atti I Congr. Intern. di Studi Fenici e Punici, Roma 1979. (= Collezioni dei studi fenici 16). Roma, 1983, 509-514. (Partly relevant) [761

Lund, J.: Sukas VIII: The Habitation Quarters (= HistFilosSkr 12 (= Publications of the Carlsberg Expedition to Phoenicia 10)). Kbh., 1986. 207 pp. [762

OTHER AREAS OF ASIA

ARABIA

Potts, D.: Trans-arabian routes of the pre-islamic period. In: L'Arabie et ses mers bordières, 1: Itinéraires et voisinages. Séminaire de recherche 1985-1986. Lyon/Paris, 1988, 127-162. (Partly relevant) [763

Potts, D.: The Arabian Gulf in antiquity. Vol. 1-2. Oxford, 1990. xxvii + 419, xxi + 369 pp. (Vol. 2 partly relevant) [764

Hannestad, L.: The Greeks in the region of the Arabian Gulf. In: Πρακτικά Α' Διεθνούς αρχαιολογικού συνεδρίου, Δελφοι 6-9 Νοεμβρίου 1986. Athenai, 1991, 41-55. [765

ICARUS

Mathiesen, H.E.: Ikaros: The Hellenistic Settlements. Vol. 1: The Terracotta Figurines (= Jysk Arkæologisk Selskabs skrifter 16:1). Århus, 1982. 93 pp. [766

Hannestad, L.: Ikaros: The Hellenistic Settlements. Vol. 2 : The Hellenistic Pottery from Failaka. With a Survey of Hellenistic Pottery in the Near East. 1-2 (= Jysk Arkæologisk Selskabs skrifter 16:2). Århus, 1983. 140, 128 pp. [767

Hannestad, L.: Danish Archaeological Excavations on Failaka. In: Arabie orientale, Mésopotamie et Iran Méridional de l'age du fer au début de la période islamique (Réunion de travail, Lyon, 1982). Paris, 1984, 59-66. – On the Hellenistic fortress. [768

Jeppesen, K.: Ikaros: The Hellenistic Settlements. Vol. 3: The sacred enclosure in the Early Hellenistic Period : with an appendix on epigraphical finds (= Jysk Arkæologisk Selskabs skrifter 16:3). Århus, 1989. 122 pp. [769

Jeppesen, K.: Zur Ergänzung, Bestimmung und Datierung der Monumentalbauten des Hellenistischen Tempelbezirks auf der Insel Ikaros/Failaka. In: Akten XIII Intern. Kongr. für Klassische Archäologie, Berlin 1988. Mainz, 1990, 324-325. [770

AFRICA

AFRICA ROMANA

Carthage

Dietz, S. & Trolle, S. (eds.): Premier rapport préliminaire sur les Fouilles Danoises à Carthage (= Working Papers of the National Museum of Denmark 10). Kbh., 1979. 146 pp. [771

Lund, J. et al.: Découvertes d'objets en céramique et de pièces de monnais. In: Dietz & Trolle, Premier rapport ... <no 771>, 1979, 51-109. [772

Dietz, S.: Bref rapport archéologique. Danemark. In: CEDAC no 4, 1981, 18-19. – An earlier, short notice by S. Trolle in CEDAC 1, 1978, 9. [773

Dietz, S.: The Concrete of Carthage. In: Annual Report Aalborg Portland. Aalborg, 1985, 24-29. [774

Dietz, S.: Fouilles Danoises à Carthage 1975-1984. In: CahEtAnc 16 (= Carthage 6), 1983 [1985], 107-118. [775

Lund, J.: The Archaeological Activities of Christian Tuxen Falbe in Carthage in 1837. In: CahEtAnc 18 (= Carthage 8), 1986, 8-24. [776

Poulsen, E.: Tombs of the IVth-Vth Centuries AD in the Danish Sector at Carthage (Falbe, site no. 90). In: CahEtAnc 18 (= Cathage 8), 1986, 141-159. [777

Lund, J.: Two Late Punic Amphora-Stamps from the Danish Excavations at Carthage. In: Carthago. Acta colloquii bruxellensis habiti diebus 2 et 3 mensis Maii anni 1986. Ed. E. Lipinski. (= Studia phoenicia 6). Leuven, 1988, 101-112. (Partly relevant) [778

Segermes

Carlsen, J. & Tvarnø, H.: The Segermes Valley Archaeological Survey (Region of Zaghouan) : An Interim Report. In: L'Africa romana 7, 1990, 803-813. [779

Ørsted, P.: Municipies et économie regionale, le programme de recherche Tuniso-Danois dans le bassin de Segermes. In: Models of regional economies in antiquity and the Middle Ages to the 11th century : session B-11. Proceed. 10th Intern. Economic History Congr. Leuven, August 1990. Eds. E. Aerts, J. Andreau & P. Ørsted (= Studies in social and economic history 14). Leuven, 1990, 26-37. [780

EGYPT

Buhl, M.-L.; Dal, E.; Holck Kolding, T.: The Danish Naval Officer Frederik Ludwig Norden: his travel in Egypt 1737-38 and his Voyage ... I-II, Copenhagen 1755 with plates by Marcus Tuscher. Three chapters. Kbh., 1986. 64 pp. (Partly relevant) [781

Bülow-Jacobsen, A.: Mons Claudianus. Roman Granite-quarry and Station on the Road to the Red Sea. In: East and West <no 1180>, 1988, 159-165. [782

Bülow-Jacobsen, A.: Review of Cuvigny, H.: L'arpentage par espèces dans l'Égypte ptolémaïque ... Bruxelles 1986. In: Gnomon 60, 1988, 236-239. [783

Buhl, M.-L.: Frederik Ludwig Norden à Alexandrie en 1737 et 1738. In: Living Waters. Scandinavian Orientalistic Studies. Presented to Professor Dr. Frede Løkkegaard on his Seventy-Fifth Birthday, January 27th 1990. Copenhagen, 1990, 31-42. (Partly relevant) [784

Bender Jørgensen, L.: Textiles from Mons Claudianus. A Preliminary Report. In: Recent Danish Research ... <no 793>, 1991, 83-95. [785

Bülow-Jacobsen, A.: Review of Klein, M.: Untersuchungen zu den kaiserlichen Steinbrüchen ... Bonn 1988. In: BibO 48, 1991, 845-847. [786

ART AND ARCHAEOLOGY

Note. Items on excavations, architecture and art and archaeology in general should be sought in the topographical sections if concerned specifically with one locality. The catalogs and guides listed under DANISH MUSEUMS should be consulted as well.

Krarup, P.: Due archeologhi danesi: Georg Zoëga e Peter Oluf Brøndsted. In: Mélanges d'Histoire Ancienne et d'Archéologie offerts à Paul Collart. Lausanne, 1976, 277-284. [787

Rathje, A.: A Group of "Phoenician" Faience Anthropomorphic Perfume Flasks. In: Levant 8, 1976, 96-106. – The flasks, a common import to Etruria and the Greek world, may be of Carthagenian manufacture. [788

Mejer, J.: Welcker and Zoëga. In: Friedrich Gottlob Welcker, Werk und Wirkung (= Hermes Einzelschriften 49) 1986, 18-23. – Essentially a biography of Zoëga. [789

Poulsgaard Markussen, E.: Calculus. Computers in Classical Archaeology. Preliminary Issue. Odense, 1986. 15 pp. [790

Randsborg, K.: Between Italy and Afghanistan: Archaeological Surveys and Ancient Civilizations. In: AArch 60, 1989 [1990], 175-185. (Partly relevant) [791

Rathje, A. & Lund, J.: Danes Overseas – A Short History of Danish Classical Archaeological Fieldwork. In: Recent Danish Research ... <no 793>, 1991, 11-56. [792

Recent Danish Research in Classical Archaeology: Tradition and Renewal. Eds. T. Fischer-Hansen, J. Lund, M. Nielsen, A. Rathje (= Acta Hyperborea 3). Kbh., 1991. 409 pp. [793

GREEK (INCLUDING PREHISTORIC) ART AND ARCHAEOLOGY

Strange, J.: Caphtor/Keftiu : a new investigation (= Acta theologica Danica 14). Leiden, 1979. 227 pp. – Thesis. [794

Trolle, S.: An Egyptian Head from Camirus, Rhodes. In: AArch 49, 1978 [1979], 139-150. [795

Strøm, I.: Middle Minoan Crete. A Re-Consideration of some of Its External Relations. In: Interaction and Acculturation in the Mediterranean. Proceed. of the 2. Intern. Congr. of Mediterranean Pre- and Protohistory, Amsterdam 19.-23. November 1980. Vol I. (= Publications of the H. Frankfort Foundation 6). Amsterdam, 1980, 105-123. [796

Strøm, I.: Aspects of Minoan foreign relations, LM I – LM II. In: Minoan Thalassocracy : Myth and Reality. Proceed. III Intern. Symposium of the Swedish Institute in Athens 31 May-5 June 1982. Eds. R. Hägg, R. & N. Marinatos. Stockholm, 1984, 191-195. [797

Buhl, M.-L.: Eleven Scarabs and One Fragment of a Faience Figurine Acquired at Lindos. In: AArch 56, 1985 [1987], 197-200. [798

Dietz, S.: Some Notes on the Pattern of Foreign Influences in the B-circle of Mycenae (The Ceramic Evidence). In: Referate vom Kollokvium zur ägäischen Vorgeschichte Mannheim 20-22.2 1986 (Schriften des Deutschen Archäologen-Verbandes). Mannheim, 1987, 113-119. [799

Dietz, S.: On the Origin of the Mycenaean Civilization : Some Recent Results. In: Studies ... <no 1181>, 1988, 22-28. [800

Hallager, E.: Aspects of Long-Distance Trade in the Second Millenium B.C. In: Momenti Precoloniale nel Mediterraneo antico. Eds. E. Acquaro et al. (= Collezione di Studi Fenici 28). 1988, 91-101. – On Minoan trade routes. [801

Dietz, S.: The concept of the middle Helladic III period in a historical perspective. In: Aegaeum 3, 1989, 123-129. [802

Sørensen, L.W. & Lund, J.: Cypriot finds in Greece and Greek finds in Cyprus ca. 950-500 BC.. In: Early Society in Cyprus. Ed. E. Peltenburg. Edinburgh, 1989, 294-295. [803

ETRUSCAN AND ITALIC ART AND ARCHAEOLOGY
Strøm, I.: Problems Concerning the Origin and Early Development of the Etruscan Orientalizing Style. 1-2 (= Odense University Classical Studies 2). Odense, 1971. 318, 89 pp. – Thesis. [804

Roberts, H.S.: Five Tomb Groups in the Danish National Museum from Narce, Capena and Poggio Sommavilla. In: AArch 45, 1974 [1975], 49-106. [805

Rathje, A.: Oriental Imports in Central and Southern Italy in the Iron Age: their affinities and implications. In: Greece and Italy in the Classical World <cf. no 650>, 1979, 189-190. – Summary of paper. [806

Rathje, A.: Oriental Imports in Etruria in the Eight and Seventh Centuries B.C. : their Origins and Implications. In: Italy before the Romans. The Iron Age, Orientalizing and Etruscan Periods. Eds. D. & F. Ridgway. London, 1979, 145-183. [807

Lavrsen, J.: Weapons in Water : a European Sacrificial Rite in Italy. In: ARID 11, 1982, 7-25. – On bronze swords found in North Italian rivers. [808

Rathje, A.: I *Keimelia* orientali. In: Opus 3, 1984, 341-354. [809

Christiansen, J.: Quattro lastre di rivestimento. In: Civilta degli Etruschi. Mostra Firenze 1985. Firenze, 1985, 158. [810

Rathje, A.: L'influenza orientale nell'Etruria e Lazio nell'Orientalizzante e il suo significato. In: TribArq 1983-1984 [1985], 83-89. [811

Rathje, A.: Five ostrich eggs from Vulci. In: Italian Iron Age Artifacts in the British Museum. Ed. J. Swaddling (= Papers of the Sixth British Museum Classical Colloquium). 1986, 397-404. [812

Rathje, A.: A tridacna squamosa shell. In: Italian Iron Age Artifacts in the British Museum <cf. no 812>, 1986, 393-396. (Marginally relevant) [813

Rathje, A.: The Etruscans. 700 Years of History and Culture. Roma, 1987. 63 pp. – Translation of Etruskerne: en antik kultur gennem 700 år. Kbh. 1982 <DOAII no 609>. [814

Rathje, A.: Gli Etruschi. 700 anni di storia e cultura. Roma, 1987. 63 pp. – Translation of Etruskerne ... <cf. no 814>. [815

Riis, P.J.: Was there in Etruscan Italy an Impact of the Grand Classical Greek Style? In: Πρακτικά του XII Διεθνούς συνεδρίου κλασικής αρχαιαλογίας, <cf. no 566>, 1988, 251-255. [816

Christiansen, J.: Comments on the Iconography of some early Etruscan revetment Plaques. In: ARID 17/18, 1989, 43-51. – Summary (titled: Some Early Etruscan Revetment Plaques in the Ny Carlsberg Glyptotek) in East and West <no 1180>, 1988, 91-92. [817

Lund, J.: [Contributions to exhibition catalogue]. In: De Etrusken. Ed. H.A.G. Brijder *et al.* s'Gravenhage, 1989, 210-216. – Nos. 17, 21-22, 51, 69, 96-97, 124, 127, 138 (all objects from the Danish National Museum). [818

Rathje, A. (Russian: Ратъе, A.): Зтруски. 700 лет истории и кулътуры. Roma, 1989. 63 pp. – Translation of Etruskerne ... <cf. no 814>. [819

Rathje, A.: An exotic piece from Vulci. The Egyptian Blue pyxis in Berlin. In: Stips votiva. Papers presented to C.M. Stibbe. Amsterdam, 1991, 171-175. [820

ROMAN ART AND ARCHAEOLOGY
Andersen, F.G.: Intorno alle origini del secondo stile. In: ARID 8, 1977, 71-78. [821

Hannestad, N.: Rome – Ideology and Art. Some Distinctive Features. In: Power and Propaganda (= Mesopotamia 7). Ed. M. Trolle Larsen. Kbh., 1979, 361-390. [822

Bek, L.: Il paesaggio tra motivo di rapprasentazione visuale e modello di descrizione letteraria. In: Prospettiva 33-36, 1983/84, 387-395. [823

Hannestad, N.: Review of Hölscher, T.: Staatsdenkmal und Publikum ... Konstanz 1984. In: Gnomon 57, 1985, 582-583. [824

Hannestad, N.: Roman art and imperial policy. Århus, 1988. 481 pp. – Thesis <= DOAII no 936>. [825

Wild, J.P. & Bender Jørgensen, L.: Clothes from the Roman Empire : Barbarians and Romans. In: Arcaeological Textiles. Ed. L. Bender Jørgensen *et al.* (= Arkæologiske Skrifter 2). København, 1988, 65-98. [826

Hannestad, N.: Monumentele publice ale artei romane : program iconografic si mesaj. Vol. 1-2. Bukuresti, 1989. 275, 461 pp. – Translation of Roman art and imperial policy <no 825>. [827

Randsborg, K.: The first millennium A. D. in Europe and the Mediterranean : an archaeological essay. Cambridge, 1991. 230 pp. (Partly relevant) [828

ARCHITECTURE

GREEK (INCLUDING MINOAN) ARCHITECTURE

Mitens, K.: Teatri greci e teatri ispirati all'architettura greca in Sicilia e nell'Italia meridionale c. 350-50 a.C. : un catalogo (= ARID Supplementum 13). Roma, 1988. 176 pp. [829

Pedersen, P.: The Parthenon and the Origin of the Corinthian Capital (= Odense University Classical Studies 13). Odense, 1989. 48 pp. [830

Hallager, E.: Upper Floors in Late Minoan I Houses. In: L'habitat égéen prehistorique (= BCH Supplement 19) Paris, 1990, 281-292. [831

Hannestad, L. & Potts, D.: Temple Architecture in the Seleucid Kingdom. In: Religion ... <no 1099>, 1990, 91-124. (Partly relevant) [832

ETRUSCAN AND ITALIC ARCHITECTURE

Pavolini, C. & Rathje, A.: L'inizio dell'architettura domestica con fondamenta in pietra nel Lazio e a Ficana. In: Ficana <no 562> 1981, 75-87. [833

Melis, F. & Rathje, A.: Considerazioni sullo studio dell'architettura domestica arcaica. In: QArchEtr 8 (= ArchLaz 6), 1984, 382-395. [834

ROMAN ARCHITECTURE
Bek, L.: Antithesis : A Roman Attitude and its Changes as Reflected in the Concept of Architecture from Vitruvius to Pliny the Younger. In: Studia Romana ... <no 1177>, 1976, 154-166. [835

Bek, L.: Towards Paradise on Earth. Modern Space Conception in Architecture: A Creation of Renaissance Humanism (= ARID Supplementum 9). Odense, 1980. 375 pp 107 pls. (Of relevance is the section p. 164-203: Axes and space in antiquity: facts and assumptions) [836

Bek, L.: Questiones Convivales : The Idea of the Triclinium and the Staging of Convivial Ceremony from Rome to Byzantium. In: ARID 12, 1983, 81-107. [837

Bek, L.: "VENUSTA SPECIES" : a Hellenistic Rhetorical Concept as the Aesthetic Principle in Roman Townscape. In: ARID 14, 1985, 139-148. [838

Nielsen, I.: Considerazioni sulle prime fasi dell'evoluzione dell'edificio termale romano. In: ARID 14, 1985, 81-112. [839

Nielsen, I.: Thermae et balnea : the architecture and cultural history of Roman public baths. Vol. 1-2. Århus, 1990. 193, 212 pp. – Thesis <= DOAII no 991>. [840

SCULPTURE

Kiilerich, B.: Graeco-Roman Influence on Gandhāra Sculpture. In: East and West <no 1180>, 1988, 140-150. [841

Moltesen, M.: The use of marble analysis in collections of ancient sculpture. Some examples from the Ny Carlsberg Glyptotek. In: Classical marble. Geochemistry, technology, trade. Eds. N. Herz & M. Waelkens. Dordrecht, 1988, 433-442. [842

GREEK SCULPTURE

Moltesen, M.: A new Replica of Myron's Athena. In: ARID 6, 1971, 7-15, pls I-IX. [843

Riis, P.J.: A Colossal Athenian Pan. In: AArch 45, 1974 [1975], 124-133. – On a sculpture in the Danish National Museum, Coll. of Antiquities inv. No Abb 160. [844

Bundgaard, J.A.: Demosthenes the Victim. In: Studia Romana ... <no 1177>, 1976, 28-37. – On a relief in Trinity college, Dublin. [845

Moltesen, M.: A new Parthenon head. In: AA 1976, 53-58. – The head, in a Danish private collection, is assigned to Metope XV. [846

Fischer-Hansen, T.: Review of Holloway, R.R.: Influences and Styles in the Late Archaic and Early Classical Greek Sculpture ... Louvain 1975. In: Gnomon 50, 1978, 578-581. [847

Sørensen, L.W.: Early Archaic Limestone Statuettes in Cypriot Style : A Review of their Chronology and Place of Manufacture. In: RDAC 1978, 111-121. [848

Moltesen, M.: Two Fleeing Niobids. In: Apollo 113, 1981, 362-365. – On NCG Inv. 472 and 520. [849

Sørensen, L.W.: A female head from Arsos. In: RDAC 1981, 169-177. [850

Moltesen, M.: Membra Collecta. In: ARID 11, 1982, 27-40. – The statuettes NCG Inv. 1570-1571 identified as made in Magna Graecia ab. 440 BC. [851

Buhl, M.-L.: L'origine des sarcophages anthropoïdes phéniciens en pierre. In: Atti I Congr. Intern. di Studi Fenici e Punici <cf. no 754>, 1983, 199-202. – Suggests Greek, or Greek-inspired, origin. [852

Riis, P.J.: The so-called Lindos Kore. In: AArch 56, 1985 [1987], 184-190. [853

Buhl, M.-L.: Les sarcophages anthropoïdes phéniciens en dehors de la Phénicie. In: AArch 58, 1987 [1988], 213-221. (Partly relevant, as the sarcophagi show Greek (through Cypriote) influence)   [854

Kiilerich, B.: Physiognomics and the Iconography of Alexander the Great. In: SymbOsl 63, 1988, 51-66. – [Aristoteles] *Physiognomonica* compared to the Lysippean tradition. [855

Nielsen, A.M.: "... fecit et Alexandrum Magnum multis operibus" : Alexander the Great and Lysippos. In: AArch 58, 1987 [1988], 151-170. [856

Nielsen, A.M.: Portraits of Alexander the Great in the Dodecanese : Some Questions – Some Answers? In: Archaeology in the Dodecanese <no 443>, 1988, 218-224. [857

Poulsen, F.: Eine Hermenbüste des Olympiodoros. In: Griechische Porträts. Ed. K. Fittschen. Darmstadt, 1988, 220-223. – Translation of La collection Ustinow ..., 1920 <PAH no 2363>, pp. 21-26. [858

Poulsen, F.: Ein Porträt des Redners Hypereides. In: Griechische Porträts <cf. no 858>, 1988, 176-184. – Translation of Un portrait de l'orateur Hypéride, 1913 <PAH no 2403>. [859

Johansen, F.: The decline and fall of a Greek portrait. A fake portrait tells its story. In: Marble. Art historical and scientific perspectives on ancient sculpture. Malibu, 1990, 223-228. [860

Moltesen, M.: Una nota sul Trono Ludovisi e sul Trono di Boston. La "connection" danese. In: BdA 75, 1990, 27-46. [861

Moltesen, M.: A Doryphoros in Disguise. In: Recent Danish Research ... <no 793>, 1991, 379-401. – On Ny Carlsberg Glyptotek cat. No. 158. Addendum by Ruth Tschäpe pp. 397-399. [862

ETRUSCAN SCULPTURE
Nielsen, M.: The Lid Sculptures of Volaterran Cinerary Urns. In: Studies in the Romanization of Etruria. Ed. P. Bruun (= Acta Instituti Romani Finlandiae, 5). Roma, 1975, 263-404. [863

Nielsen, M.: I coperchi delle urne volterrane. Caratteristiche e datazione delle ultime botteghe. In: Caratteri dell'ellenismo nelle urne etrusce; Atti dell'Incontro di Studi: Università di Siena 28-30 aprile 1976. Eds. M. Martelli & M. Cristofani. Firenze, 1977, 137-141. [864

Moltesen, M.: A Charun head in Ischia di Castro. In: StEtr 46, 1978, 65-73. [865

Nielsen, M.: Immagini di artigiani? Lineamenti di uno sviluppo; La bottega e l'organizzazione del lavoro; La distribuzione nel territorio; Le produzioni locali nel territorio volterrano; Circolazione dei modelli e delle maestranze. In: Artigianato artistico in Etruria : L'Etruria settentrionale interna in età ellenistica. Ed. A. Maggiani. Milano, 1985, 26-28, 49-50, 52-66, 74-76, 117. [866

Nielsen, M.: Late Etruscan Cinerary Urns from Volterra at the J. Paul Getty Museum : A Lid Figure Altered from Male to Female, and an Ancestor to Satirist Persius. In: GettyMusJ 14, 1986, 43-58. [867

Nielsen, M.: Scultori perugini a Volterra nel I sec. a.C.? In: Atti II Congr. Intern. Etrusco. Firenze, 1989, vol. II, s. 1002-1023. [868

Rathje, A.: Alcune considerazioni sulle lastre di Poggio Civitate con figure femminili. In: Le Donne in Etruria <cf. no 410>, 1989, 75-84. [869

ROMAN SCULPTURE
Johansen, F.: Ritratti marmorei e bronzei di Marco Vipsanio Aggrippa. In: ARID 6, 1971, 17-48. [870

Hannestad, N.: The Portraits of Aelius Caesar. In: ARID 7, 1974, 67-100, pls 1-18. [871

Haarløv, B.: Un altro ritratto dell'imperatore Valeriano? In: ARID 7, 1974, 101-108. [872

Haarløv, B.: New Identifications of Third Century Roman Imperial Portraits (= Odense University Classical Studies 7). Odense, 1975. 26 pp 51 pls. [873

Gjødesen, M.: A Fragment of the Arch of Titus. In: Studia Romana ... <no 1177>, 1976, 72-86. – On a frieze fragment deposited in the Ny Carlsberg Glyptotek. [874

Haarløv, B.: A Contribution to the Iconography of the Emperor Gallienus. In: Studia Romana ... <no 1177>, 1976, 113-121. [875

Johansen, F.: Le Portrait d'Auguste de Prima Porta et sa datation. In: Studia Romana ... <no 1177>, 1976, 49-57. [876

Riis, P.J.: An Aeneas in the Ny Carlsberg Glyptotek? In: In memoriam Otto J. Brendel. Essays in archaeology and the humanities. Eds. L. Bonfante & H. v. Heintze. 1976, 165-171. [877

Hannestad, N.: The Liberalitas Panel of Marcus Aurelius once again – is Herodes Atticus represented on it? In: ARID 8, 1977, 79-88. [878

Hannestad, N.: Review of Kruse, H.J.: Römische weibliche Gewandstatuen ... Göttingen 1975. In: JRS 67, 1977, 220. [879

Hannestad, N.: Review of Zanker, P. Klassizistische Statuen ... Mainz 1974. In: JRS 67, 1977, 221-222. [880

Haarløv, B.: The Half-Open Door : A Common Symbolic Motif within Roman Sepulchral Sculpture (= Odense University Classical Studies 10). Odense, 1977. 174 pp, 40 pls. – Thesis. [881

Johansen, F.: Ritratti antichi di Cicerone e Pompeo Magno. In: ARID 8, 1977, 39-69. [882

Haarløv, B.: The half-open door – a common symbolic motif within Roman sepulchral art. In: Greece and Italy in the Classical World <cf. no 650>, 1979, 271. – Summary of paper. Cf. no 881. [883

Johansen, F.: A Republican and an Emperor. In: Apollo 113, 1981, 366-368. [884

Johansen, F.: Antike Porträts von Caligula in der Ny Carlsberg Glyptotek. In: WZBerlin 31, 1982, 223-224. [885

Fejfer, J.: The portraits of the Severan Empress Julia Domna: A new approach. In: ARID 14, 1985, 129-138. – On the use of inscriptional evidence. [886

Johansen, F.: The Portraits in Marble of Gaius Julius Caesar: A Review. In: Ancient Portraits in the J. Paul Getty Museum, 1. Malibu, 1987, 17-40. [887

Johansen, F.: The Sculpted Portraits of Caligula. In: Ancient Portraits ... <cf. no 887>, 1987, 87-106. [888

Fejfer, J.: Official Portraits of Julia Domna. In: Ritratto Ufficiale e Ritratto Privato. Atti II confer. intern. sul Ritratto Romano, Roma 1984 (= Quaderni de la Ricerca Scientifica 116). Roma, 1988, 295-301. [889

Hannestad, N.: The so-called Daughter of Marcus Aurelius or some Remarks on Late Roman Sculpture. In: Studies ... <no 1181>, 1988, 195-203. [890

Haarløv, B.: Ny Carlsberg Glyptotek Cat. no. 467. Emperor or philosopher? In: Ritratto Ufficiale e Ritratto Privato <cf. no 889>, 1988, 319-323. [891

Fejfer, J. & Southworth, E.: Summer in England. Ince Blundell Hall revisited. In: Apollo 129, 1989, 179-182. [892

Hannestad, N.: Review of Andreae, B. & Conticello, B.: Skylla und Karybdis ... Stuttgart 1987. In: Gnomon 61, 1989, 655-657. [893

Hannestad, N.: The Classical Tradition in Late Roman Sculpture. In: Akten XIII Intern. Kongr. für Klassische Archäologie <cf. no 770>, 1990, 516-517. [894

Kiilerich, B.: A head of a boy in Oslo : Theodosius' grandson? In: IstMitt 40, 1990, 201-206. [895

Kiilerich, B. & Torp, H.: A Christ and the apostles relief in search of a date. In: Arte Medievale, II Ser, 4:1, 1990, 99-115. [896

Moltesen, M.: The Aphrodisian sculptures in the Ny Carlsberg Glyptotek. In: Aphrodisias Papers. Recent Work on Architecture and Sculpture. Ed. C. Roueché (= JRA Supplement 1). Ann Arbor, 1990, 133-146. [897

Fejfer, J. & Southworth, E.: The Ince Blundell Collection of classical sculpture, 1. The portraits, 1. Introduction. The female portraits. Concordances (= Corpus signorum imperii romani. Great Britain 3,2). London, 1991. 97 pp, 25 pls. [898

Moltesen, M.: Neue Nasen, neue Namen. In: AA 1991, 271-279. – On NCG cat. nos. 597, 655, 631, 630, 635, 602, 614. [899

POTTERY

Johansen, F.: Una trozzella Messapica alla gliptoteca Ny Carlsberg di Copenhaghen. In: AC 24, 1972, 256-262, pls.. [900

Hannestad, L.: The Paris Painter : An Etruscan Vase-Painter (= HistFilolMed 47, 2). Kbh., 1974. 51 pp, 34 pls. – Addenda in Followers ... <no 904> p. 81-83. [901

Dietz, S.: Two Painted Duck-Vases from Rhodos. In: AArch 45, 1974 [1975], 133-143. [902

Fischer-Hansen, T.: Yet Another Human Sacrifice? In: Studia Romana ... <no 1177>, 1976, 20-27. – On an Etruscan crater, Cervetri inv. 19539. [903

Hannestad, L.: The followers of the Paris Painter (= HistFilolMed 47, 4). Kbh., 1976. 95 pp, 59 pls. – Section on the Silen Painter (p. 34-46) in collaboration with Anja Drukker. P. 81-83 Addenda to The Paris Painter <no 901>. [904

Moltesen, M.: An Etruscan Olla. In: Studia Romana ... <no 1177>, 1976, 6-9. – On a 7th cent. BC impasto vessel in the Accademia di Danimarca, Rome. [905

Rathje, A.: Some Unusual Vessels with Plastic Heads on their Necks. In: Studia Romana ... <no 1177>, 1976, 10-19. – On stone, ivory and pottery vessels from Etruria. [906

Rafn, B.: The Corinthian Chimaera Group, its chronology and relations with Protocorinthian and Attic Pottery. In: AArch 49, 1978 [1979], 151-190. [907

Roberts, H.S.: Etruscan Bucchero with Incised Decoration. In: Greece and Italy in the Classical World <cf. no 650>, 1979, 192. – Summary of paper. [908

Roberts, H.S.: The Tomb Group From Poggio Sommavilla in the Danish National Museum. In: Civiltà arcaica dei Sabini nella valle del Tevere, III; Rilettura critica della necropoli di Poggio Sommavilla. Ed. Consiglio Nazionale delle Ricerche; Centro di Studio per l'Archeologia Etrusco-Italica. Roma, 1977 [1980], 49-74. [909

Christiansen, J.: A Panathenaic Price Amphora. In: Apollo 113, 1981, 358-361. [910

Ginge, B.: The erotic hare : a hare-shaped Etruscan plastic vase in the Odense University classical collection (= Skrifter udgivet af Institut for klassiske studier). Odense, 1981. 39 pp. [911

Nielsen, A.M.: A pictorial vase in Milwaukee. In: RDAC 1981, 154-156. – On a Cypro-Archaic I oinochoe and other vessels from the same workshop. [912

Strøm, I.: Review of Rasmussen, T.B.: Bucchero Pottery from Southern Etruria. Cambridge 1979. In: Gnomon 53, 1981, 789-792. [913

Rathje, A.: A Banquet Service from the Latin City of Ficana. In: ARID 12, 1983, 7-29. [914

Christiansen, J.: Did the Kleophon-Painter make Panathenaics? In: Ancient Greek and Related Pottery <cf. no 452>, 1984, 144-148. [915

Christiansen, J.: A Pair of Amphorae from Caere. In: ARID 13, 1984, 7-23. – On Ny Carlsberg Glyptotek HIN 679 and 680. [916

Hannestad, L.: The Pottery from the Hellenistic Settlements on Failaka. In: Arabie orientale ... <cf. no 768>, 1984, 67-83. [917

Hannestad, L.: Slaves and the Fountain House Theme. In: Ancient Greek and Related Pottery <cf. no 452>, 1984, 252-255. [918

Sørensen, L.W.: Three Cypro-Archaic I Vases Decorated with Birds. In: RDAC 1984, 162-168. [919

Liventhal, V.: What Goes On among the Women? – the Setting of some Attic Vase Paintings of the Fifth Century B.C. In: ARID 14, 1985, 37-52. – The hydria Inv. 7359 in the National Museum interpreted as a prize in a competition of Pyrrhic dancing. [920

Beltov, F.: Metrological Aspects of Greek Vases: An Examination of Measurements and Capacities compiled from Jaap Hemelrijk's Publication 'Caeretan Hydriae'. In: Hephaistos 7/8, 1985/86, 125-151. [921

Hannestad, L.: Two Eye Cups from the Workshop of Lydos. In: Studien zur Mythologie und Vasenmalerei. Konrad Schauenburg zum 65. Geburtstag ... Mainz, 1986, 41-46. [922

King, R.H.; Rupp, D.W.; Sørensen, L.W.: A Multivariate Analysis of Pottery from Southeastern Cyprus using Neutron Activation Analysis. In: JAS, 1986, 361-374. (Partly relevant) [923

Roberts, H.S.: Aspects of the Archaic Animal Style on Pottery found in Etruria and the Faliscan Area. In: Italian Iron Age Artifacts in the British Museum <cf. no 812>, 1986, 419-430. [924

Ginge, B.: Ceramiche etrusche a figure nere (= Archeologia 72 (= Materiali del Museo archeologico nazionale di Tarquinia 12)). Roma, 1987. 117 pp. [925

Hallager, E.: The Inscribed Stirrup Jars : Implications for Late Minoan II B Crete. In: AJA 91, 1987, 171-190. [926

Sørensen, L.W.: Cypriote Iron Age Pottery. An Experiment Employing simple Quantitative Analysis. In: SIMA 77, 1987, 129-135. (Marginally relevant) [927

Dietz, S.; Nordquist, G.; Zerner, C.: Concerning the Classification of Late Middle Helladic Wares in the Argolid. In: HYDRA (Athens) 5, 1988, 15-16. [928

Ginge, B.: Etruscan black-figured vases in the Archaeological Museum of Tarquinia. Addenda. In: AnnPerugia 26, 1988, 59-85. [929

Ginge, B.: A New Evaluation of the Origins of Tyrrhenian Pottery : Etruscan Precursors of Pontic Ceramics. In: Proceedings ... <no 936>, 1988, 201-210. [930

Hallager, B.P.: Mycenaean Pottery in Late Minoan IIIA:1 Deposits at Khania, Western Crete. In: Problems in Greek Prehistory. Papers presented at the Centenary Conference of the British School of Archaeology at Athens, Manchester April 1986. Eds. E.B. French & K.A. Wardle. Bristol, 1988, 173-183. [931

Hannestad, L.: The Athenian Potter and the Home Market. In: Proceedings ... <no 936>, 1988, 222-230. [932

Jeppesen, K.: On the Interpretation of the Principal Scene on the Krater Schloss Fasanerie no 77 by the Kekrops Painter. In: Proceedings ... <no 936>, 1988, 285. [933

Lund, J. & Rathje, A.: Italic Gods and Deities on Pontic Vases. In: Proceedings ... <no 936>, 1988, 352-366. [934

Moltesen, M.: A Group of Late-Etruscan Silver-Imitating Vases. In: Proceedings ... <no 936>, 1988, 435-444. [935

Proceedings of the 3rd Symposium on Ancient Greek and Related Pottery, Copenhagen August 31-September 4 1987. Eds. J. Christiansen and T. Melander. Kbh., 1988. 683 pp. [936

Sørensen, L.W.: Greek Pottery from the Geometric to the Archaic Period found on Cyprus. In: East and West <no 1180>, 1988, 12-32. [937

Hannestad, L.: Athenian pottery in Etruria c. 550-470 B.C. In: AArch 59, 1988 [1989], 113-130. [938

Hannestad, L.: The Castellani fragments in the Villa Giulia : Athenian black figure, Vol. 1. Århus, 1989. viii + 162 pp. [939

Ginge, B.: Etruscan mortuary symbolism. Oriental influences on Polychrome Group ceramics. In: Die Welt der Etrusker <cf. no 642>, 1990, 231-240. [940

Ginge, B.: Oriental Influences on Etruscan Polychrome Ceramics : the Evidence from Satricum. In: ARID 19, 1990, 7-24. [941

Ginge, B.: Recent study of Etruscan ceramics. In: JRA 3, 1990, 225-233. – Review article of Martelli, M. (ed.): La ceramica degli etruschi ... Novara 1987; of Spivey, N.J.: The Micali Painter ... Oxford 1987, and of Rizzo, M.A.: Un artista etruscho ... Roma 1988. [942

Hannestad, L.: Change and Conservatism: Hellenistic Pottery in Mesopotamia and Iran. In: Akten XIII Intern. Kongr. für Klassische Archäologie <cf. no 770>, 1990, 179-186. [943

Hannestad, L.: Review of Leach, S.S.: Subgeometric pottery from southern Etruria. Göteborg 1987. In: Gnomon 62, 1990, 144-147. [944

Bundgaard Rasmussen, B.: Laconian Pottery in the National Museum, Copenhagen. In: Recent Danish Research ... <no 793>, 1991, 321-335. [945

Ginge, B.: Review of Leach, S.S.: Subgeometric Pottery from Southern Etruria. Göteborg 1987. In: AJA 95, 1991, 550. [946

Rafn, B.: Two Laconian black-glazed Droop cups from Haleis. In: Stips votiva <cf. no 820>, 1991, 163-169. [947

Roberts, H.S.: A New Bucchero Kantharos with Incised Frieze Found at Vulci. In: Recent Danish Research ... <no 793>, 1991, 337-363. [948

Slej, K.: Hellenistic Black-glaze Ware from the Temple of Castor and Pollux in the Forum Romanum : The Stamps. In: Recent Danish Research ... <no 793>, 1991, 249-268. [949

Sørensen, L.W.: Three Corinthian Sherds from Rhodes : A Case Study. In: Recent Danish Research ... <no 793>, 1991, 191-205. [950

Hannestad, L.: Athenian Pottery in Corinth c. 600-470 B.C. In: AArch 62, 1991 [1992], 151-163. [951

TERRACOTTAS, IVORIES

Fischer-Hansen, T.: Some Sicilian arulae and their significance. In: ARID 8, 1977, 7-18. [952

Riis, P.J.: Etruscan Types of Heads : a Revised Chronology of the Archaic and Classical Terracottas of Etruscan Campania and Central Italy (= Hist-FilosSkr 9:5). Kbh., 1981. 84 pp. [953

Hvidberg-Hansen, F.O.: Due arule fittili di Solunto. In: ARID 13, 1984, 25-48. [954

Lund, J.: A Fake Roman Terracotta-Lamp Found at Søsum, Denmark. In: AArch 57, 1986 [1987], 229-232. – In the table of contents called A Forged .... [955

Kiilerich, B. & Torp, H.: Hic est: hic Stilicho. The date and interpretation of a notable diptych. In: JdI 104, 1989, 319-371. – The diptych is dated to 395-402. [956

Kiilerich, B.: A different interpretation of the Nicomachorum-Symmachorum diptych. In: JAC 34, 1991, 115-128. [957

Lund, J.: Towards a Better Understanding of the Production Pattern of Roman Lamps. In: Recent Danish Research ... <no 793>, 1991, 269-295. [958

Sørensen, L.W.: Cypriote Terracottas from Lindos in the Light of New Discoveries. In: Cypriote Terracottas, Proceed. of the First Intern. Confer. of Cypriote Studies. Bruxelles-Liège, 1991, 225-240. [959

Østergaard, J.S.: Terracotta Horses and Horsemen of Archaic Boeotia. In: Recent Danish Research ... <no 793>, 1991, 111-189. [960

GEMS AND SEALINGS

Jeppesen, K.: Neues zum Rätsel des Grand Camée de France (= Acta Jutlandica 44:1). Århus, 1974. 95 pp. [961

Hallager, E. & Vlasakis, M.: Two new roundels with Linear A from Khania. In: Kadmos 23, 1984, 1-10. [962

Hallager, E.: The Master Impression : a clay sealing from the Greek-Swedish excavations at Kastelli, Khania (= SIMA 69). Göteborg, 1985. 75 pp. [963

Hallager, E.: The Knossos Roundels. In: BSA 82, 1987, 55-70. [964

Hallager, E.: On the Track of Minoan Bureaucrats and their 'Clients'. In: Ειλαπίνη. Τόμος τιμητικὸς γιὰ τὸν καθηγητὴ Νικόλαο Πλάτωνα. Heraklion, 1987, 347-353. [965

Tzedakis, Y. & Hallager, E.: A clay-sealing from the Greek-Swedish excavations at Khania. In: The Function of the Minoan Palaces <cf. no 577>, 1987, 117-120. [966

Hallager, E.: The Roundel in the Minoan Administrative System. In: Problems in Greek Prehistory <cf. no 931>, 1988, 101-112. – Summary published in East and West <no 1180>, p. 9-11. [967

Hallager, E.: The Use of Seals on the Minoan Roundel. In: Fragen und Probleme der Bronzezeitlichen ägäischen Glyptik; 3. Intern. Marburger Symposium (= CMS Beiheft 3). Marburg, 1988, 55-78. [968

Hallager, E.; Godart, L.; Olivier, J.-P.: La rondelle en linéaire A d'Haghia Triada Wc 3024 (HM 1110). In: BCH 113, 1989, 431-437. − From Haghia Triada, Cyprus. [969

Hallager, E.: Roundels among Sealings in Minoan Administration : A Comprehensive Analysis of Function. In: Aegaeum 5, 1990, 121-142. − Discussion p. 143-147. [970

BRONZES, OTHER METALWORK, AND GLASS

Johansen, F.: Reliefs en bronze d'Étrurie. Kbh., 1971. 166 pp, 67 pls. [971

Bruhn Hoffmeyer, A.: Arms and armour in Spain. A short survey, I: The Bronze Age to the end of High Middle Age. Jariz de la Vera (Cáceres), 1972. 199 pp. + 118 pls. (Of relevance is the section pp. 56-65: Weapons of Hisperia Romana) [972

Dietz, S.: Aegean and Near-Eastern Metal Daggers in Early and Middle Bronze Age Greece : The Dating of the Byblite Hoards and Aegean Imports. In: AArch 42, 1971 [1972], 1-22. [973

Jeppesen, K. : An Inside View of the Hoby Cups. In: AArch 43, 1972 [1973], 1-18. [974

Poulsen, E.: Probleme der Werkstattbestimmung gegossener römischer Figuralbronzen. Herstellungsmilieu und Materialstruktur. In: AArch 48, 1977 [1978], 1-60. [975

Melander, T.: Some late Etruscan Mirrors in the Thorvaldsen Museum. In: Bronzes héllenistiques et romains. Tradition et renouveau. Actes V Colloque intern. sur les bronzes antiques, Lausanne 8-13 mai 1978 (= Cahiers d'Archéologie Romande 17). Lausanne, 1979, 161-167. [976

Poulsen, E.: The Manufacture of Final Models of Roman Mass Produced Pail Handle Attachments. In: Bronzes héllenistiques et romains <cf. no 976>, 1979, 241-245. [977

Roberts, H.S.: Etruscan Mirrors of the Hellenistic Period. In: Bronzes héllenistiques et romains <cf. no 976>, 1979, 157-160. [978

Rathje, A.: Silver Relief Bowls from Italy. In: ARID 9, 1980, 7-46. [979

Johansen, F.: Etruscan Engraved Plaques. In: Apollo 113, 1981, 356-357. [980

Roberts, H.S.: Later Etruscan Mirrors. Evidence for Dating from Recent Excavations. In: ARID 12, 1983, 31-54. [981

Poulsen, E.: Über Massenherstellung römischer Bronzestatuetten. Dublettenserien und Modellverhältnisse. In: Toreutik und figürliche Bronzen römischer Zeit. Akten der 6. Tagung über antike Bronzen, 13.-17.Mai 1980. Ed. E. Gehrig. Berlin, 1984, 207-215. [982

Lith, S.M.E. van & Randsborg, K.: Roman Glass in the West. A social study. In: BerOudBod 35, 1985, 413-532. [983

Strøm, I.: Decorated bronze sheets from a chair. In: Italian Iron Age Artifacts in the British Museum <cf. no 812>, 1986, 53-62. [984

Munksgaard, E.: Spätantikes Silber. In: FMS 21, 1987, 82-84. – On the treasure find at Gudme, Fyn. [985

Roberts, H.S.: On the Interpretation of Mirror Supports from Southern Italy and Greece. Four Examples in the Danish National Museum. In: Griechische und römische Statuetten und Grossbronzen. Akten der 9. intern. Tagung über antike Bronzen. Wien 21.-25.April 1986. Ed. K. Gschwantler *et al.* Wien, 1988, 249-257. [986

Roberts, H.S.: Some Observations on Etruscan Bowls with Supports in the shape of Caryatids or Adorned by Reliefs. In: East and West <no 1180>, 1988, 69-80. [987

Lund Hansen, U.: Römischer Glasexport in das freie Germanien. In: KölnJb 22, 1989, 177-185. (Marginally relevant) [988

Strøm, I.: Orientalising Bronze Reliefs from Chiusi. In: ARID 17/18, 1989, 7-27. [989

Melander, T.: Eine Meisterbronze aus dem archaischen Griechenland. In: Akten XIII Intern. Kongr. für Klassische Archäologie <cf. no 770>, 1990, 461-462. – On a bronze handle in Thorvaldsens Museum, Inv 2273. [990

Strøm, I.: Die Bronzethronlehne aus Chiusi. Staatliche Museen zu Berlin, DDR, Inv. M.I. 8383. In: Die Welt der Etrusker <cf. no 642>, 1990, 139-142. [991

Ginge, B.: Review of Meer, L.B. van der: The bronze liver of Piacenza ... Amsterdam 1987. In: AJA 95, 1991, 557. [992

Roberts, H.S.: Un Mercurio de bronce hallado en Sagunt. In: Saguntum y El Mar. Ed. C. Aranegui Gascó. Valencia, 1991, 32-33. [992a

Poulsen, E.: Römische Bronzeeimer. Typologie der Henkelattachen mit Frauenmaske, Palmette und Tierprotomen. In: AArch 62, 1991 [1992], 209-230. [993

NUMISMATICS

Mørkholm, O.: The Danish Contribution to the Study of Ancient Numismatics 1780-1880. In: Den Kongelige Mønt- og Medaillesamling 1781-1981. København, 1981, 123-129. [994

Kromann, A.: Western Features in the Kushan Coinage. In: East and West <no 1180>, 1988, 151-158. [995

GREEK NUMISMATICS
Mørkholm, O.: Une trouvaille de monnaies grecques archaïques. In: SNR 50, 1971, 79-91. [996

Olçay, N. & Mørkholm, O.: The Coin Hoard from Podlia. In: NC 11, 1971, 1-29. – The hoard comprises mostly Lycian coins. [997

Mørkholm, O.: A Hellenistic Coin Hoard from Bahrain. In: Kuml 1972, 195-202. [998

An Inventory of Greek Coin Hoards. Eds. M. Thompson, O. Mørkholm, and C.M. Kraay. New York, 1973. xviii + 408 pp. [999

Mørkholm, O. & Zahle, J.: The Coinage of Kuprlli : Numismatic and Archaeological Study. In: AArch 43, 1972 [1973], 57-113. [1000

Mørkholm, O.: A Coin of Artaxerxes III. In: NC 14, 1974, 1-4. – On imitations of Attic Owls. [1001

Mørkholm, O.: A Further Comment on the Coinage of Ariarathes VIII and Ariarathes IX. In: NAC 4, 1975, 109-139. [1002

Mørkholm, O.: Ptolemaic Coins and Chronology. The Dated Silver Coinage of Alexandria. In: ANSMN 20, 1975, 7-24. [1003

Mørkholm, O.: The Ptolemaic "Coins of an Uncertain Era". In: NNÅ 1975-76, 23-58. [1004

Christiansen, E.: The Roman coins of Alexandria. A Preliminary Report. In: Actes VIII Congr. Intern. de Numismatique <cf. no 426>, 1976, 243-252. [1005

Mørkholm, O.: Hellenistic coin hoards from the Persian Gulf. In: Actes VIII Congr. Intern. de Numismatique <cf. no 426>, 1976, 123. [1006

Nikolau, I.; Mørkholm, O.: Paphos I. A Ptolemaic Coin Hoard. Nicosia, 1976. x + 115 pp, 22 pls. [1007

Christiansen, E.: Review of Geissen, A.: Katalog Alexandrinischer Kaisermünzen der Sammlung des Instituts für Altertumskunde ... Köln, 1 ... Opladen 1974. In: JRS 67, 1977, 207-208. [1008

Mørkholm, O. & Zahle, J.: The Coinages of the Lycian Dynasts Kheriga, Kherâi and Erbbina. In: AArch 47, 1976 [1977], 47-90. [1009

Mørkholm, O.: A Summary of Recent Scholarship. Additions and Corrections. In: Newell, E.T: Western Seleucid Mints. Reprint New York, 1977, i-ix. – Also printed p. i-ix in Newell, E.T. Eastern Seleucid Mints. Repr. New York 1978. [1010

Mørkholm, O. & Neumann, G.: Die lykischen Münzlegenden (= NachrAkGött 1978,1. Göttingen, 1978. 38 pp, 4 pls. [1011

Mørkholm, O.: The Alexander Coinage of Nicocles of Paphos. In: Chiron 8, 1978, 135-147. [1012

Mørkholm, O.: The Coinages of Ariarathes VI and Ariarathes VII of Cappadocia. In: SNR 57, 1978, 144-163. [1013

Mørkholm, O.: The Era of the Pamphylian Alexanders. In: ANSMN 23, 1978, 69-75. [1014

Christiansen, E.: Review of Gara, A.: Prosdiagraphomena e circolazione monetaria ... Milano 1976. In:
JRS 69, 1979, 204-206. [1015

Mørkholm, O.: The Cappadocians Again. In: NC 139, 1979, 242-246. [1016

Mørkholm, O.: The Hellenistic Period. Greece to India. In: A Survey of Numismatic Research 1972-77. Bern, 1979, 60-97. [1017

Mørkholm, O.: A Hoard of Coins from Characene. In: CoinH 4, 1979, 26-27. [1018

Mørkholm, O.: New Coin Finds from Failaka. In: Kuml 1979, 230-236. – Danish version, Nye møntfund fra Failaka pp. 219-229 (not in DOAI). [1019

Mørkholm, O.: The Portrait Coinage of Ptolemy V. The Main Series. In: Greek Numismatics and Archaeology. Essays in Honor of Margeret Thompson. Eds. O. Mørkholm and N. Waggoner. Wetteren, 1979, 203-214. [1020

Mørkholm, O.: Some Reflections on the Early Cistophoric Coinage. In: ANSMN 24, 1979, 47-61. [1021

Thompson, Margeret ; Mørkholm, O.; Kraay, C.M.: An Inventory of Greek Coin Hoards. A Discussion. In: AIIN 23-24, 1976-1977 [1979], 319-323. – Reply to L. Breglia's comments on no 999 in AIIN 21-22 (1974-75 [1977]), 215-222. [1022

Mørkholm, O.: A History of the Study of Greek Numismatics. I-II c.1780-c.1870. III c. 1870-1940. In: NNÅ 1979-80, 5-21; NNÅ 1982, 7-26. [1023

Christiansen, E.: Apis III : A Critical Note. In: ARID 9, 1980, 75-77. [1024

Mørkholm, O.: Chronology and Meaning of the Wreath Coinages of the Early 2nd Century B.C. In: NAC 9, 1980, 145-158. [1025

Mørkholm, O.: Cyrene and Ptolomy I. Some Numismatic Comments. In: Chiron 10, 1980, 145-159. [1026

Mørkholm, O.: A Group of Ptolemaic Coins from Phoenicia and Palestine. In: INJ 4, 1980, 4-7. [1027

Mørkholm, O.: Sculptures and Coins. The Portrait of Alexander Balas of Syria. In: NAC 10, 1981, 235-245. [1028

Mørkholm, O.: Some Coins of Ptolemy V from Palestine. In: INJ 5, 1981, 5-10. [1029

Mørkholm, O.: The Attic Coin Standard in the Levant During the Hellenistic Period. In: Studia Paolo Naster oblata I (= Orientalia Lovaniensia 12). Louvain, 1982, 139-149. [1030

Mørkholm, O.: The "Behaviour" of Dies in the Hellenistic Period. In: Proceed. IX Intern. Congr. of Numismatics, Bern 1979. Louvain-La-Neuve, 1982, 209-214. [1031

Mørkholm, O.: Some Reflections on the Production and Use of Coinage in Ancient Greece. In: Historia 31, 1982, 290-305. [1032

Zahle, J.: Persian Satraps and Lycian Dynasts. The Evidence of the Diadems. In: Proceed. IX Intern. Congr. of Numismatics <cf. no 1031>, 1982, 101-112. [1033

Mørkholm, O.: The Last Ptolemaic Silver Coinage in Cyprus. In: Chiron 13, 1983, 69-79. [1034

Mørkholm, O.: The Life of Obverse Dies in the Hellenistic Period. In: Studies in Numismatic Methods Presented to Phillip Grierson. Cambridge, 1983, 11-21. [1035

Mørkholm, O.: A Posthumous Issue of Antiochus IV of Syria. In: NC 143, 1983, 57-63. [1036

Mørkholm, O.: The Ptolemaic Coinage in Phoenicia and the Fifth War with Syria. In: StHell 27, 1983, 241-251. [1037

Mørkholm, O.: The Autonomous Tetradrachms of Laodicea ad Mare. In: ANSMN 28, 1983, 87-107. [1038

Mørkholm, O.: Two Cypriot Coins of Antiochus IV of Syria. In: Cyprus Numismatic Society Numismatic Report 12, 1981 [1983], 51-53. [1039

Christiansen, E.: On Denarii and other Coin-Terms in the Papyri. In: ZPE 54, 1984, 271-299. [1040

Mørkholm, O.: The Alleged Portrait of Antiochus, Son and Co-Regent of Antiochus the Great. In: NC 144, 1984, 184-186. [1041

Mørkholm, O.: The Chronology of the New Style Coinage of Athens. In: ANSMN 29, 1984, 29-42. [1042

Mørkholm, O.: The Monetary System in the Seleucid Empire after 187 BC. In: Ancient Coins in the Graeco-Roman World; The Nickle Numismatic Papers. Eds. W. Heckel & R. Sullivan. Toronto, 1984, 93-113. [1043

Mørkholm, O. & Kromann, A.: The Ptolemaic Silver Coinage on Cyprus 192/1-164/3. In: Chiron 14, 1984, 149-165. [1044

Mørkholm, O.: Some Pergamene Coins in Copenhagen. In: Studies in Honor of Leo Mildenberg. Wetteren, 1984, 181-192. [1045

Christiansen, E.: The Roman Coins of Alexandria (30 B.C. to A.D. 296). An inventory of hoards. In: CoinH 7, 1985, 77-140. [1046

Mørkholm, O.: Sylloge nummorum Graecorum. Deutschland: Sammlung v. Aulock. Vol. 11: Pamphylien. West Milford, N.J., 1986. 5 pp, 14 pls. (Reprint of the edition Berlin, 1965 <=PAH no 2682>). [1047

Mørkholm, O.: Cyprus Hoard, 1982. In: NC 147, 1987, 156-158. [1048

Mørkholm, O.: The Date of the Autonomous Tetradrachms of Aegae in Cilicia. In: ANSMN 32, 1987, 57-60. [1049

Christiansen, E.: The Roman coins of Alexandria. Quantitative Studies. Nero, Trajan, Septimius Severus. Vol. 1-2. Århus, 1988. 311, 197 pp. – Thesis <= DOAII no 1098>. [1050

Christiansen, Erik: From Zoëga to the Present Day. The Roman Coins of Alexandria in 200 Years of Research. In: Studies ... <no 1181>, 1988, 232-242. (Partly relevant) [1051

Kromann, A.: Greek and Phoenician Letters on Aradian Tetradrachms. In: Studies ... <no 1181>, 1988, 104-113. [1052

Kromann, A.: The Greek Imperial Coinage from Cos and Rhodes. In: Archaeology in the Dodecanese <no 443>, 1988, 213-217. [1053

Christiansen, E.: Review of Förschner, G.: Die Münzen der römischen Kaiser in Alexandrien ... Frankfurt a.M. 1987. In: NC 149, 1989, 242-243. [1054

Jensen, J.S.: The Bibliography of Otto Mørkholm 1930-1983. In: Kraay-Mørkholm essays : numismatic studies in memory of C.M. Kraay and O. Mørkholm. Louvain-la-Neuve, 1989, xv-xix. – The bibliography includes posthumously published material up to 1987. [1055

Kromann, A.: Marks of Value on Greek Imperials from Side. In: Kraay-Mørkholm essays <cf. no 1055>, 1989, 149-158. [1056

Zahle, J.: Politics and economy in Lycia during the Persian period. In: REA 91, 1989, 167-182. – On coin circulation within and outside Lycia. [1057

Christiansen, E.: On the avoidance of *Theta* on Alexandrian Coins. In: Proceed. X Intern. Congr. of Numismatics, London September 1986. Ed. I.A. Carradine (= International Association of Professional Numismatists; Publication 11). Maastricht, 1990, 231-238. [1058

Zahle, J.: Herrscherporträts auf lykischen Münzen. In: Götter, Heroen, Herscher in Lykien (Ausstellungskatalog, Schloss Schallaburg, Österreich). Wien/München, 1990, 51-57, 172-179. [1059

Zahle, J.: Lycian Coin Portraits. Forerunners of the Hellenistic Portraits of Rulers on Coins. In: Akten XIII Intern. Kongr. für Klassische Archäologie <cf. no 770>, 1990, 568-569. [1060

Zahle, J.: Religious Motifs on Seleucid Coins. In: Religion ... <no 1099>, 1990, 125-139. [1061

Christiansen, E.: Coins of Alexandria and the Nomes : a supplement to the British Museum catalogue (= Occasional paper; British Museum 77). London, 1991. vii + 151 pp, 12 pls. [1062

Christiansen, E.: The Roman Coins of Alexandria (30 B.C. to A.D. 296). A survey of collections. In: NNÅ 1983-84 [1991], 5-58. [1063

Mørkholm, O.: Early Hellenistic coinage from the accession of Alexander to the peace of Apamea (336 – 188 B.C.). Eds. by P. Grierson and U. Westermark. Cambridge, 1991. 273 pp. [1064

ROMAN NUMISMATICS
Bay, Aa.: The letters SC on Augustean aes coinage. In: JRS 62, 1972, 111-122. [1065

Thomsen, R.: Early Roman coinage. A study of the chronology. Vol. 1: The evidence (= Nationalmuseets skrifter. Arkæologisk-historisk række 5). Kbh., 1974. 251 pp. (Reprint of the edition Kbh. 1957 <PAH no 2716>, vol. 1). [1066

Thomsen, R.: From Libral 'Aes Grave' to Uncial 'Aes' Reduction. The Literary Tradition and the Numismatic Evidence. In: Les devaluations à Rome (= CEFR 137). Rome, 1978, 9-22. [1067

Kromann, A.: Die römischen Münze von Gudme. In: FMS 21, 1987, 61-73. [1068

Kromann, A.: A fourth-century hoard from Denmark. In: RIN 90, 1988, 239-259. [1069

Kromann, A.: Recent Roman Coin Finds from Denmark. In: Proceed. X Intern. Congr. of Numismatics <cf. no 1058>, 1990, 263-274. [1070

DANISH MUSEUMS

Note. Single museum pieces or groups of pieces should be sought in the sections under ART AND ARCHAEOLOGY

Roberts, H.S.: Corpus speculorum Etruscorum. Denmark 1: Copenhagen, The Danish National Museum, The Ny Carlsberg Glyptothek (= Corpus speculorum Etruscorum, Denmark: 1; fasc. 1). Odense, 1981. 132 pp. [1071

Mathiesen, H.E.: Sylloge Nummorum Graecorum: Aarhus University, Denmark. Kbh., 1986. 44 pls. [1072

Mathiesen, H.E.: Sylloge Nummorum Graecorum: The Fabricius Collection, Aarhus University, Denmark, and the Royal Collection of Coins and Medals, Danish National Museum, Copenhagen. Ed. H.E. Mathiesen. Kbh., 1987. 21 pls. – Of the collection, 396 coins are kept in Aarhus University, 110 in the National Museum. [1073

Gundestrup, B.: Egyptian, Greek and Roman Antiquities in the Oldest Royal Kunstkammer Collection in Denmark. In: The Classical Heritage ... <no 1182>, 1990, 43-56. [1074

THE NATIONAL MUSEUM
Sylloge Nummorum Graecorum. The Royal Collection of Coins and Medals, Danish National Museum. Vol. 41 : Alexandria-Cyrenaica. Eds. E. Christiansen and A. Kromann. Kbh., 1974. 31 pls. – Nos 1-1163 (Alexandria and the Nomes) by E. Christiansen; nos 1164-1322 (Cyrene) by A. Kromann. [1075

Sylloge Nummorum Graecorum. The Royal Collection of Coins and Medals, Danish National Museum. Vol. 40 : Egypt: The Ptolemies. Eds. O. Mørkholm and A. Kromann. Kbh., 1977. 22 pls. [1076

Sylloge Nummorum Graecorum. The Royal Collection of Coins and Medals, Danish National Museum. Vol. 43: Spain-Gaul. Eds. G.K. Jenkins and A. Kromann. Kbh., 1979. 9 pp, 39 pls. [1077

Mørkholm, O.: The Royal Collection of Coins and Medals 1780/81-1980/81. In: Compte rendu de la Commission intern. de numismatique 27, 1980, 31-42. [1078

Sylloge Nummorum Graecorum. The Royal Collection of Coins and Medals, Danish National Museum. Vol. 1-8. West Milford, N.J., 1981-1982, vol. 8 1992. 8 vols.. (Reprint of the edition 1942-1979 <PAH no 2737 and nos 1075-1077 in present bibliography>).
The reprint comprises:
Vol. 1, Italy-Sicily (=fasc. 1-5)
Vol. 2, Thrace and Macedonia (= fasc. 6-10)
Vol. 3, Greece: Thessaly to Aegean Islands (=fasc. 11-17)
Vol. 4, Bosporus to Lesbos (=fasc. 18-21)
Vol. 5, Ionia, Caria and Lydia (=fasc. 22-28)
Vol. 6, Phrygia to Cilicia (=fasc. 29-33)
Vol. 7, Cyprus to India (=fasc. 34-39)
Vol. 8, Egypt, North Africa, Spain-Gaul (=fasc. 40-43) [1079

Riis, P.J.; Moltesen, M.; Guldager, P.: The National Museum of Denmark. Catalogue of ancient sculptures, 1: Aegean, Cypriote, and Graeco-Phoenician (= Publications of The Department of Near Eastern and Classical Antiquites, The National Museum of Denmark). Kbh., 1989. 115 pp. [1080

Riis, P.J.: Schliemann und Dänemark. In: Resümees zur internat. Tagung Heinrich Schliemann – Grundlagen und Ergebnisse moderner Archäologie. Berlin, 1990, 102-104. – Final publication in: Heinrich Schliemann – Grundlagen und Ergebnisse moderner Archäologie 100 Jahre nach Schliemanns Tod, Berlin 1990. Berlin 1992, p. 133-139. (Maginally relevant) [1081

Kromann, A.: Sestini and the private collection of King Christian VIII. In: Ermanno A. Arslan studia dicata, vol 3. Milano, 1991, 779-788. [1082

THE NY CARLSBERG GLYPTOTHEK

Poulsen, V.: Ny Carlsberg Glyptotek : A guide to the collections. 15th ed. revised by Flemming Johansen. Kbh., 1972. 118 pp. – Revised edition of PAH no 2747. Later revised editions: 16th, 1976; 17th, 1981; 18th, 1983. [1083

Poulsen, V.: Les portraits romains. Vol. 1: République et dynastie Julienne (= Publications de la Glyptothèque Ny Carlsberg 7). Kbh., 1973. 158 pp, 204 pls. (Reprint of the edition Kbh. 1962 <PAH no 2759>). [1084

Poulsen, V.: Les portraits romains : Vol. 2. De Vespasien à la basse-antiquité. Traduit du danois par Ghani Merad. Texte.-Planches. 1974 (= Publications de la Glyptothèque Ny Carlsberg 8). Kbh., 1974. 220 pp, 353 pls. [1085

Nielsen, A.M.: Cypriote antiquities in the Ny Carlsberg Glyptotek, Copenhagen (= SIMA 20:8 (= Corpus of Cypriote antiquities 8)). Gothenburg, 1983. 47 pp. – Includes Roman glass in addition to earlier Cypriote material. [1086

Østergaard, J.S.: Antikens ansikte. Grekiska og romerska porträtt från Ny Carlsberg Glyptotek, Köpenhamn. Kbh., 1986. 56 pp. – Exhibition catalogue. Danish edition 1990 <DOAII no 1135>. [1087

Moltesen, M.: From the Princely Collections of the Borghese Family to the Glyptotek of Carl Jacobsen. In: ARID 16, 1987, 187-203. [1088

Moltesen, M.: Brewer Carl Jacobsen's Thoughts on Ancient Sculpture and Its Communication. In: The Classical Heritage ... <no 1182>, 1990, 251-265. [1089

Moltesen, M. & Weber-Lehmann, C.: Catalogue of the Copies of Etruscan Tomb Paintings in the Ny Carlsberg Glyptotek. Kbh., 1991. 157 pp. [1090

THORVALDSEN'S MUSEUM
Melander, T.: Thorvaldsen e la cultura archeologica. In: Bertel Thorvaldsen, 1770-1844, scultore danese a Roma. Ed. E. di Majo. Roma, 1989, 284-307. (Partly relevant, including a catalogue of antiquities in Thorvaldsen's Museum) [1091

RELIGION AND MYTHOLOGY

Note. Artistic representation of mythological subjects should be sought in the relevant sections on ART AND ARCHAEOLOGY.

Asmussen, J.P.: Der Mithraskult. In: Handbuch der Religionsgeschichte. Herausgeb. von J.P. Asmussen und J. Læssøe in Verbindung mit C. Colpe. Vol. 3, Göttingen, 1975, 301-308. – Translation of Mithraskulten <PAH no 2836>, in Asmussen and Læssøe: Illustreret Religionshistorie 1-3, Kbh., 1968, of which the *Handbuch* is a translation. [1092

Giversen, S.: Der Gnostizismus und die Mysterienreligionen. In: Handbuch der Religionsgeschichte; Vol. 3 <cf. no 1092>, 1975, 255-299. – Translation of Gnosticismen ... <PAH no 2835>. [1093

Iversen, E.: Egyptian and Hermetic doctrine (= Opuscula Graecolatina 27). Kbh., 1984. 71 pp. [1094

Hansen, J. V.: Adamas and the Four Illuminators in Sethian Gnosticism. In: Rethinking Religion <no 1097>, 1989, 55-71. (Marginally relevant) [1095

Podemann Sørensen, J.: The Myth of Attis: Structure and Mysteriosophy. In: Rethinking Religion <no 1097>, 1989, 23-29. [1096

Rethinking Religion : Studies in the Hellenistic Process. Ed. J.Podemann Sørensen (= Opuscula Graecolatina 30). Kbh., 1989. 101 pp. [1097

Bilde, P.: Atargatis/Dea Syria: Hellenization of Her Cult in the Hellenistic-Roman Period? In: Religion ... <no 1099>, 1990, 151-187. [1098

Religion and Religious Practice in the Seleucid Kingdom. Eds. P. Bilde, T. Engberg-Pedersen, L. Hannestad and J. Zahle (= Studies in Hellenistic Civilization 1). Århus, 1990. 269 pp. (Partly relevant) [1099

See also no 92

GREEK RELIGION AND MYTHOLOGY

Jensen, P.J.: Die griechische Religion. In: Handbuch der Religionsgeschichte; Vol. 3 <cf. no 1092>, 1975, 135-217. – Translation of Græsk religion <PAH no 2915>. [1100

Prytz Johansen, J.: The Thesmophoria as a women's festival. In: Temenos 11, 1975, 78-87. [1101

Hansen, O.: The ring-inscription from Ezerovo and the origin of the Ares-cult. In: Eranos 86, 1988, 69-70. [1102

Sørensen, V.: Apollons uppror : de odödligas historia. Stockholm, 1989. 123 pp. – Translation of Apollons oprør : de udødeliges historie. Kbh. 1989 <DOAII no 1195>. [1103

Sørensen, V.: I begynnelsen var Eros : de udødeliges historie. Oslo, 1989. 121 pp. – Translation of Apollons oprør <cf. no 1103>. [1104

Skafte Jensen, M.: Helena: Die schöne H. In: Enzyklopädie des Märchens, Vol. 6 <cf. no 128>, 1990, 765-767. [1105

Sørensen, V.: Apolls Aufruhr : die Geschichte der Unsterblichen. München, 1991. 150 pp. – Translation of Apollons oprør <cf. no 1103>. [1106

ROMAN RELIGION AND MYTHOLOGY

Vanggaard, J.H.: On Parilia. In: Temenos 7, 1971, 91-103. [1107

Jensen, P.J.: Die römische Religion. In: Handbuch der Religionsgeschichte; Vol. 3 <cf. no 1092>, 1975, 219-253. – Translation of Romersk religion <PAH no 2985>. [1108

Vanggaard, J.H.: The October Horse. In: Temenos 15, 1979, 81-95. – On the horse sacrifice on Idus oct. [1109

Christensen, T.: Christus oder Jupiter : der Kampf um die geistigen Grundlagen des Römischen Reiches. Göttingen, 1981. 295 pp. – Translation of Romermagt, hedenskab og kristendom. Kbh., 1970 <DOAI no 717>. [1110

Vanggaard, J.H.: The Flamen. A study in the history and sociology of Roman religion. Kbh., 1988. 175 pp. – Thesis <= DOAII no 1197>. [1111

Bilde, P.: The Meaning of Roman Mithraism. In: Rethinking Religion <no 1097>, 1989, 31-47. [1112

Podemann Sørensen, J.: Attis or Osiris? Firmicus Maternus, *De errore* 22. In: Rethinking Religion <no 1097>, 1989, 73-86. – On 4th cent. AD syncretism. [1113

PHILOSOPHY

Note. Subdived in General, Presocratics, Socrates, Peripatetics, Stoics, Epicureans. For philosophers whose works survive whole or in part, see AUTHORS AND TEXTS.

GENERAL
Mejer, J.: Review of Reale, G.: Melisso Testimonizianze e Frammenti. Firenze 1970, and of Coutant, V. (ed.): Theophrastus De Igne ... Assen 1971. In: RMeta 28, 1974, 132-133, 139-140. [1114

Ebbesen, S.: Hoc aliquid – quale quid and the signification of appellatives. In: Philosophia 5/6, 1975/76, 370-392. (Partly relevant, spanning from Aristotele to Wittgenstein) [1115

Ebbesen, S.: Review of Nuchelmans, G.: Theories of the Proposition ..., Amsterdam 1973. In: Lingua 40, 1976, 89-97. (Partly relevant) [1116

Ebbesen, S.: Suprasegmental Phonemes in Ancient and Mediaeval Logic. In: English Logic and Semantics from the End of the Twelfth Century to the Time of Ockham and Burleigh. Acts of the 4th European Symposium on Mediaeval Logic and Semantics. Eds. H.A.G. Braakhuis *et al.* (= Artistarium, Supplement 1). Nijmegen, 1981, 331-359. (Partly relevant) [1117

Ebbesen, S.: Ancient scholastic logic as the source of mediaeval scholastic logic. In: The Cambridge History of Later Mediaeval Philosophy. Cambridge, 1982, 101-127. (Partly relevant) [1118

Ebbesen, S.: The Odyssey of Semantics from the Stoa to Buridan. In: History of Semiotics. Eds. A. Eschbach & J. Trabant. (= Foundations of Semiotics 7). Amsterdam, 1983, 67-85. (Partly relevant) [1119

Ebbesen, S.: The Chimera's Diary. In: The Logic of Being. Eds. S. Knuuttila & J. Hintikka. Dordrecht, 1986, 115-143. (Partly relevant, treating the logical problem of reference – implying existence – to imaginary beings, from the sophists to Buridan and Ockham) [1120

Ostenfeld, E.[N.]: Ancient greek psychology and the modern mind-body debate. Århus, 1987. 109 pp. – Thesis. [1121

Ebbesen, S.: Les Grecs et l'ambiguïté. In: L'ambiguïté: Cinq études historiques. Ed. I. Rosier. Lille, 1988, 15-32. [1122

Larsen, Ø.: Ethik und Demokratie : die Entstehung des ethischen Denkens im demokratischen Stadtstaat Athen. Hamburg, 1990. 151 pp. – Translation of Den etiske tænkemådes tilblivelse i den demokratiske bystat Athen. Roskilde, 1986 <DOAII no 1228>. [1123

THE PRESOCRATICS
Mejer, J.: Plato, Protagoras and the Heracliteans. In: C&M 29, 1968 [1972], 40-60. [1124

Mejer, J.: Review of Hussey, E.: The Presocratics. London 1972. In: RMeta 27, 1974, 797-798. [1125

Mejer, J.: Review of Newiger, H.J.: Untersuchungen zur Gorgias' Schrift Über das Nichtseiende, Berlin 1973; of Mourelatos, A.P.D. (ed.): The Presocratics, Garden City, N.Y. 1974, and of Allen, R.E. & Furley, D.J. (eds.): Studies in Presocratic Philosophy II, London 1975. In: CW 70, 1977, 275, 398-399. [1126

Democritus
Friis Johansen, K.: The Concept of Nature in Democritus. In: DYPhilos 23, 1986, 148-167. [1127

Protagoras
Mejer, J.: The Alleged New Fragment of Protagoras. In: Hermes 100, 1972, 175-178. – Repr. in Classen, C.J. (ed.): Sophistik (= Wege der Forschung 187). Darmstadt, 1976, 306-311. [1128

Foss, O.: The Pigeon's Neck. In: Classica ... <no 1176>, 1973, 140-149. – Demonstrates that the category πρός τί is wrongly ascribed to Protagoras in Elias' commentary on Aristotle's Categories. [1129

Bernsen, N.O.: Protagoras' Homo-Mensura Thesis. In: C&M 30, 1969 [1974], 109-144. [1130

Pythagoras, Pythagoreans
Ostenfeld, E.[N.]: Early Pythagorean Principles; Peras and Apeiron. In: Ionian Philosophy. Ed. K.J. Boudouris. Athens, 1989, 304-311. [1131

SOCRATES
Hjortsø, L.: The Point Between the Thaw and the Frost. In: Classica ... <no 1176>, 1973, 629-635. – On Socratic irony. [1132

See also no 174

PERIPATETICS

Ebbesen, S.: The Contribution of the Greek Commentators on the *Organon* to the Formation of Western Scholasticism. In: Proceed. of the World Congr. on Aristotle, Thessaloniki August 7-14, 1978; Vol. I. Athens, 1981, 183-186. (Partly relevant) [1133

Ebbesen, S.: Philoponus, 'Alexander' and the origins of mediaeval logic. In: Aristotele Transformed <cf. no 188>, 1990, 445-461. (Marginally relevant) [1134

STOICS

Christensen, J.: Equality of Man and Stoic Social Thought. In: Equality and Inequality of Man in Ancient Thought. Ed. I. Kajanto (= Commentationes Humanarum Litterarum 75). Helsingfors, 1984, 45-54. [1135

Ebbesen, S.: Semantics – Stoic, Late Ancient, and Medieval. In: Zeichen und Realität. Ed. K. Oehler. Tübingen, 1984, 383-388. (Partly relevant) [1136

Engberg-Pedersen, T.: Discovering the good: *oikeiosis* and *kathekonta* in Stoic Ethics. In: The Norms of Nature, Studies in Helllenistic Ethics. Eds. M. Schofeld & G. Striker. Cambridge, 1986, 145-183. [1137

Engberg-Pedersen, T.: Review of Inwood, B.: Ethics and Human Action in Early Stoicism. Oxford 1986. In: PhR 97,2, 1988, 252-256. [1138

Engberg-Pedersen, T.: Stoic Philosophy and the Concept of the Person. In: The Person and the Human Mind: Issues in Ancient and Modern Philosophy. Ed. C. Gill. Oxford, 1990, 109-135. [1139

Engberg-Pedersen, T.: The Stoic Theory of Oikeiosis : Moral Development and Social Interaction in Early Stoic Philosophy (= Studies in Hellenistic Civilization 2). Århus, 1990. 278 pp. [1140

EPICUREANS

Mejer, J.: Review of Bollack, J. & Laks, A.: Études sur l'épicurisme antique. Lille 1976. In: Gnomon 51, 1979, 641-645. [1141

SCIENCE AND TECHNOLOGY

Pedersen, O. & Pihl, M.: Early physics and astronomy. A historical introduction. New York, 1974. 417 pp. (Relevant section pp. 11-169 on Greek science) [1142

Blomqvist, J.: Review of J.Barnes *et al.* (eds.): Science and Speculation ... Cambridge 1982. In: Lychnos, 1984, 240-242. [1143

MATHEMATICS, INCLUDING ASTRONOMY

Aaboe, A.: Remarks on the theoretical treatment of eclipses in antiquity. In: JHA 3, 1972, 105-118. [1144

Pedersen, O.: Logistics and the theory of functions. An essay in the history of Greek mathematics. In: AIHS 24, 1974, 29-50. [1145

Moesgaard, K.P.: Elements of Planetary, Lunar and Solar Orbits, 1900 B.C. to A.D. 1900, Tabulated for Historical Use. In: Centaurus 19, 1975, 157-181. (Marginally relevant) [1146

Moesgaard, K.P.: Hipparchus' solar theory derived from lunar eclipse observations – resumé. In: JHA 7, 1976, 216-217. [1147

Taisbak, C.M.: Ante Diem : Did the Romans count their days backwards? In: Studia Romana ... <no 1177>, 1976, 58-59. [1148

Taisbak, C.M.: Review of Horowitz, Th.: Vom Logos zur Analogie ... Zürich 1978. In: Centaurus 25, 1981/82, 334-335. [1149

Esrom Larsen, M.: On the Possibility of a Pre-Euclidian Theory of Proportions. In: Centaurus 27, 1984, 1-25. [1150

Moesgaard, K.P.: Synodic Period Relations in Babylonian and Hellenistic Astronomy. In: Vistas in Astronomy 28, 1985, 119-121. (Partly relevant) [1151

Andersen, K.: Ancient Roots of Linear Perspective. In: From Ancient Omens to Statistical Mechanics <cf. no 197>, 1987, 75-89. – On Euclid, Ptolemaios and Vitruvius. [1152

Høyrup, J.: Dynamis and Mithartum. On Analogous Concepts in Greek and Old Babylonian Mathematics (= FilRUCPrep 1988 Nr. 1). Roskilde, 1988. 38 pp. – Demonstrates that Dynamis may signify the square, as well as the root/side of the square. [1153

Høyrup, J.: On Parts of Parts and Ascending Continued Fractions. An Investigation on the Origins and Spread of a Peculiar System (= FilRUCPrep 1988 Nr. 2). Roskilde, 1988. 26 pp. – Final publication in Centaurus 33, 1990, p. 293-324. (Marginally relevant, touching (p.4-5) on arithmetical riddles in Anthologia Graeca XIV) [1154

Høyrup, J.: Dynamis, the Babylonians, and Theaetetus 147c7-148d7. In: HM 17, 1990, 201-222. – On the mathematical concept Dynamis <cf. no 1153>. [1155

Høyrup, J.: Sub-scientific Mathematics: Undercurrents and Missing Links in the Mathematical Technology of the Hellenistic and Roman World (= FilRUCPrep 1990 Nr. 3). Roskilde, 1990. 55 pp. – Preprint of contribution to ANRW II, 37, 5. [1156

MEDICINE

Nielsen, H.: Ancient ophthalmological agents. A pharmacohistorical study of the collyria and seals for collyria used during Roman antiquity, as well as of the most frequent components of the collyria (= Acta Historica Scientiarum Naturalium et Medicinalium 31). Odense, 1974. 116 pp. – Translation of Oldtidens øjenmedicin. Kbh., 1973 <DOAI no 1048>. [1157

Brøndegaard, V.J.: Das Wurzelstechen. In: ZWG 67, 1983, 199-209. – On the grafting of vegetable stalks as a veterinary remedy; the procedure is attested to by Columella. [1158

Nielsen, H.: Medicaments used in the treatment of eye diseases in Egypt, the countries of the Near East, India and China in antiquity. Odense, 1987. 76 pp. (P. 22-24 marginally relevant) [1159

TECHNOLOGY

Drachmann, A.G.: The Crank in Graeco-Roman Antiquity. In: Changing Perspectives in the History of Science, Essays in Honour of Joseph Needham. London, 1973, 33-51. [1160

Drachmann, A.G.: Review of Krafft, F.: Dynamische und statische Betrachtungsweise ... Wiesbaden 1970. In: Centaurus 17, 1973, 330-335. [1161

Schiøler, T.: Roman and Islamic Water-Lifting Wheels (= Acta Historica Scientiarum Naturalium et Medicinalium 28). Odense, 1973. 200 pp. – Thesis. (Partly relevant) [1162

Drachmann, A.G.: Ktesibios' Waterclock and Heron's Adjustable Siphon. In: Centaurus 20, 1976, 1-10. [1163

Drachmann, A.G.: Biton, and the Development of the Catapult. In: ΠΡΙΣ-MATA. Naturwissenschaftgeschichtliche Studien. Festschrift für Willy Hartner. Wiesbaden, 1977, 119-131. [1164

Raasted, J.: A Neglected Version of the Anecdote about Pythagoras's Hammer Experiment. In: CIMAGL 31, 1979, 1-9. – On acoustics. [1165

Schiøler, T.: Bronze Roman Piston Pumps. In: HTech 5, 1980, 17-38. [1166

Schiøler, T.: Note di antica technologia idraulica. In: Comune di Roma: Il trionfo dell'acqua. Roma, 1986, 157-163. [1167

Schiøler, T.: Power Adjustment before James Watt. In: Polhem 4, 1986, 191-201. (Partly relevant) [1168

Drachmann, A.G.: Antikens teknik : om den västerländska civilisationens första tekniska hjälpmedel. Stockholm, 1988. 143 pp. (Reprint of the edition

Stockholm 1965 <PAH no 3155>). – Translation of Antikkens teknik. Kbh., 1961 <PAH no 3154>. [1169

Schiøler, T.: Rekonstruktion einer römischen Feuerlöschpumpe im Antiquarium Comunale. In: MittLeichtweiss 103, 1989, 281-313. [1170

Schiøler, T. & Garcia-Diego, J.A.: Bronze Roman piston pumps. In: Ancient Technology. Symposium Athens 30.3 – 4.4 1987 (= Tekniikan museom julkaisuja, 5). Helsinki, 1990, 46-67. – Revised version of no 1166. [1171

HISTORY OF DANISH CLASSICAL SCHOLARSHIP

Jensen, P.J.: J.N.Madvig. Avec une esquisse de l'histoire de la philologie classique au Danemark (= Odense University Classical Studies 12). Odense, 1981. 282 pp. [1172

Mejer, J.: Wilamowitz and Scandinavia: Friendship and Scholarship. In: Wilamowitz nach 50 Jahren. Eds. W.M. Calder III et al. Darmstadt, 1985, 511-537. (Marginally relevant) [1173

Mejer, J.: Madvig, J.N. In: Classical Scholarship. A Biographical Encyclopedia. Eds. W.M.Calder III & W.W. Briggs. New York/London, 1990, 260-263. [1174

GENERALIA ET COLLECTANEA

Bibliography
Hansen, P.A.: A Bibliography of Danish Contributions to Classical Scholarship from the Sixteenth Century to 1970 (= Danish Humanist Texts and Studies 1). Kbh., 1977. xviii + 335 pp. [1175

Collections

Classica et mediaevalia Francisco Blatt septuagenario dedicata. Eds. O.S. Due, H. Friis Johansen, B. Dalsgaard Larsen (= C&M Dissertationes 9). Kbh., 1973. 676 pp. [1176

Studia Romana in Honorem Petri Krarup Septuagenarii. Eds. K. Ascani, T. Fischer-Hansen, F. Johansen, S. Skovgaard Jensen, J.E. Skydsgaard. Odense, 1976. 248 pp. [1177

Madvig, J.N.: Opuscula Academica. Hildesheim, 1977. xi + 779 pp. (Facsimile of the edition Kbh. 1887 <PAH no 3212>). [1178

Hansen, P.A.: Review of Jensen, P.J.: Cum grano salis ... Odense 1981. In: CR 33, 1983, 378. – The reviewed work is in Danish <DOAII no 1> and falls outside the scope of the present bibliography, but the review raises an interesting point of principle. [1179

East and West : Cultural Relations in the Ancient World. Ed. T. Fischer-Hansen (= Acta Hyperborea 1). Kbh., 1988. 167 pp. [1180

Studies in Ancient History and Numismatics presented to Rudi Thomsen. Eds. A. Damsgaard-Madsen, E. Christiansen and E. Hallager. Århus, 1988. 270 pp. [1181

The Classical Heritage in Nordic Art and Architecture. Acts of the Seminar held at the University of Copenhagen, 1st-3rd November 1988. Ed. M. Nielsen (= Acta Hyperborea 2). Kbh., 1990. 300 pp. (Partly relevant) [1182

Other general works

Smith, O.L.: Review of Irmscher, J. *et al.*: Einleitung in die klassischen Altertumswissenschaften ... Berlin 1986. In: Philologus 134, 1990, 290-293. [1183

INDEX ANNORUM

1934:   367

1937:   367a

1963:   368

1969:   101

1970:   161

1971:   1, 81, 102, 112, 116, 162, 177, 323, 355, 386, 387, 392, 393, 616, 661, 804, 843, 870, 971, 996, 997, 1107

1972:   2, 30, 130, 134, 153, 158, 167, 175, 199, 216, 277, 283, 289, 424, 458, 696, 749, 752, 900, 972, 973, 998, 1065, 1083, 1124, 1128, 1144

1973:   12, 32, 82, 87, 95, 111, 113, 131, 137, 163, 168, 176, 200, 278, 290, 425, 459, 578, 603, 705, 742, 758, 974, 999, 1000, 1084, 1129, 1132, 1160-1162, 1176

1974:   3, 17, 19, 23, 39, 72, 88, 117, 154, 164, 169, 183, 185, 187, 189, 193, 237, 302, 349, 354, 388, 430, 460, 553, 604, 645, 665, 706, 871, 872, 901, 961, 1001, 1066, 1075, 1085, 1114, 1125, 1130, 1142, 1145, 1157

1975:   4-6, 21, 31, 33, 60, 135, 170, 238, 239, 272, 273, 291, 292, 303, 350, 401, 426, 444, 461, 462, 605, 707, 724, 805, 844, 863, 873, 902, 1002-1004, 1092, 1093, 1100, 1101, 1108, 1115, 1146

1976:   7, 8, 34, 73, 74, 89, 103, 178, 201, 203, 240, 279, 293, 417, 426, 427, 431, 445, 463-465, 554, 666, 708, 725, 726, 759, 787, 788, 835, 845, 846, 874-877, 903-906, 1005-1007, 1116, 1147, 1148, 1163, 1177

Index Annorum

1977: 106, 136, 151, 241, 288, 294, 369, 380, 446, 466-468, 575, 579, 626, 646-648, 709, 727, 728, 821, 864, 878-882, 952, 1008-1010, 1076, 1126, 1164, 1175, 1178

1978: 13, 35, 61, 75, 97, 110, 242, 295, 304, 324-326, 379, 418, 469-471, 576, 580, 649, 658, 699, 710, 711, 760, 773, 847, 848, 865, 975, 1010-1014, 1067

1979: 14, 15, 43, 47, 118, 138, 186, 219, 243, 244, 327, 328, 394, 447, 472-476, 555, 556, 627, 631, 650, 712, 729, 771, 772, 794, 795, 806, 807, 822, 883, 907, 908, 976-978, 1015-1023, 1077, 1109, 1141, 1165

1980: 18, 22, 27, 48, 114, 122, 147, 155, 204, 220, 228, 229, 245, 296, 319, 329, 330, 358, 395, 432, 433, 441, 448, 477-480, 598, 600, 610a, 651, 662, 667, 730, 796, 836, 909, 979, 1024-1027, 1078, 1166

1981: 9, 44, 51, 83, 84, 94, 107, 114, 123, 142, 145, 156, 190, 246, 247, 331, 332, 351, 365, 481-487, 581, 627, 633, 643, 652-655, 659, 693, 713, 773, 833, 849, 850, 884, 910-913, 953, 980, 994, 1028, 1029, 1071, 1079, 1110, 1117, 1133, 1149, 1172

1982: 10, 52, 57, 62, 63, 90, 104, 108, 109, 139, 171, 217, 230, 231, 248, 305, 306, 333-336, 356, 357, 396, 449, 488, 489, 557, 558, 582, 617, 618, 639, 663, 664, 743, 766, 808, 851, 885, 1030-1033, 1118

1983: 28, 36, 40, 64-66, 124, 202, 249, 250, 274, 284, 297, 307, 381, 397, 434, 490-499, 559, 583-585, 619, 627, 639, 668-671, 714-716, 731, 734, 761, 767, 823, 837, 852, 914, 981, 1034-1039, 1086, 1119, 1158, 1179

1984: 67, 96, 165, 194, 205, 206, 232, 251-253, 275, 308, 309, 337, 363, 370, 408, 419, 450-452, 500-503, 560, 571, 586, 609, 611, 613, 630, 634, 644, 672, 673, 735, 768, 797, 809, 834, 915-919, 954, 962, 982, 1040-1045, 1094, 1135, 1136, 1143, 1150

1985: 41, 68, 179, 191, 192, 195, 254-257, 338-341, 371, 382, 383, 398, 399, 409, 428, 453, 504-508, 561-563, 572, 587, 588, 620, 640, 656, 674, 675, 753, 757, 774, 775, 810, 811, 824, 838, 839, 866, 886, 920, 921, 963, 983, 1046, 1151, 1173

1986: 11, 24, 26, 53, 69, 85, 125, 144, 146, 150, 172, 180, 181, 205, 209, 221, 225, 298, 299, 310-312, 342, 352, 359, 360, 384, 509-511, 564, 573, 589, 590, 676, 697, 717, 744, 751, 754, 762, 776, 777, 781, 789, 790, 812, 813, 867, 922-924, 984, 1047, 1072, 1087, 1120, 1127, 1137, 1167, 1168

1987: 25, 29, 54, 76, 93, 98, 121, 126, 132, 140, 148, 152, 196, 197, 214, 222, 226, 227, 233, 234, 258-260, 270, 271, 285, 313, 314, 343, 372, 373, 389, 402, 404, 420, 512-519, 565, 577, 591, 592, 606, 612, 621, 635, 660, 677, 678, 736, 737, 798, 799, 814, 815, 853, 887, 888, 925-927, 955, 964-966, 985, 1048, 1049, 1068, 1073, 1088, 1121, 1152, 1159

1988: 16, 37, 49, 50, 58, 77, 78, 99, 115, 133, 141, 143, 159, 207, 210, 218, 234, 261-263, 315, 320, 344, 385, 390, 405, 406, 410, 421-423, 435-437, 443, 520-527, 566, 567, 574, 593-595, 610, 612, 614, 622, 636, 679-683, 700, 718-720, 745, 746, 763, 778, 782, 783, 800, 801, 816, 817, 825, 826, 829, 841, 842, 854-859, 889-891, 928-937, 967, 968, 986, 987, 995, 1050-1053, 1069, 1102, 1111, 1122, 1138, 1153, 1154, 1169, 1180, 1181

1989: 59, 70, 86, 91, 92, 127, 157, 160, 208, 211, 215, 223, 224, 235, 264-266, 280-282, 286, 321, 345, 346, 353, 361, 374, 400, 411, 412, 442, 454, 528-539, 568, 569, 596, 601, 607, 637, 638, 684-686, 694, 695, 698, 701, 703, 721, 750, 769, 802, 803, 817-819, 827, 830, 868, 869, 892, 893, 938, 939, 956, 969, 988, 989, 1054-1057, 1080, 1091, 1095-1097, 1103, 1104, 1112, 1113, 1131, 1170

1990: 38, 42, 45, 54, 55, 71, 79, 80, 100, 105, 119, 128, 129, 166, 173, 184, 188, 212, 276, 300, 316, 322, 362, 364, 375, 376, 391, 403, 413-415, 429, 438, 455, 540-548, 570, 597, 599, 612a, 615, 623, 628, 632, 642, 657, 687-690, 692, 702, 704, 722, 747, 755, 764, 770, 779, 780, 784, 791, 831, 832, 840, 860, 861, 894-897, 940-944, 970, 990, 991, 1058-1061, 1070, 1074, 1081, 1089, 1098, 1099, 1105, 1123, 1134, 1139, 1140, 1154-1156, 1171, 1174, 1182, 1183

1991:   20, 46, 56, 79, 120, 149, 174, 182, 198, 213, 236, 267-269, 287, 301, 317, 318, 347, 348, 366, 377, 378, 407, 416, 439, 440, 456, 457, 549-552, 602, 608, 624, 625, 629, 641, 691, 723, 732, 733, 738-741, 748, 756, 765, 785, 786, 792, 793, 820, 828, 862, 898, 899, 945-950, 957-960, 992, 992a, 1062-1064, 1082, 1090, 1106

1992:   951, 993, 1079

INDEX OF AUTHORS

Algreen-Ussing, Gregers (1938-) 605, 656, 657
Almar, Knud Paasch (1935-) 322
Andersen, Elga (1934-) 598
Andersen, Flemming Gorm (1946-) 620, 699, 751, 757, 821
Andersen, Helle Damgaard (1960-) 632
Andersen, Kirsti (1941-) 196, 1152
Andersen, Lene (1940-) 117, 389, 390
Andreanaki-Vlasaki, M. – see: Vlasakis
Ascani, Karen (1940-) 1177
Asmussen, Jes P. (1928-2002) 1092
Axelson, B. 215
Balling, A.K. – see: Kromann, A.
Bartolini, G. 646, 648, 649
Bay, Aase (1942-1971) 1065
Becker, M. 684
Bek, Lise (1936-) 183, 823, 835-838
Bekker-Nielsen, Tønnes (1955-) 435, 694, 698, 738
Beltov, Finn (1922-) 921
Bender Jørgensen, Lise (1949-) 785, 826
Bendtsen, Margit (1948-) 570
Bendz, Gerhard (1908-1985) 57, 82, 110, 386, 387, 392, 393
Bernsen, Niels Ole (1942-) 1130
Bilde, Per (1939-) 138-141, 418, 1098, 1099, 1112

Bjertrup, Lars (1956-) 508, 539, 541, 552
Blomqvist, Jerker (1938-) 108, 144, 152, 298, 356, 357, 365, 1143
Boserup, Ivan (1944-) 162
Bramsnæs, Annelise (1941-1999) 605
Brandt, R. 652
Brashear, W.M. 347
Breitenstein, Thorkild (1936-) 116
Bro, Thyge C. (1955-) 772
Bruhn Hoffmeyer, Ada (1910-1991) 972
Bruun, Niels Wilhelm (1944-) 209, 210, 212, 215, 226, 236, 237, 240, 245, 246, 280, 320, 321, 372, 375
Brøndegaard, Vagn J. (1919-) 1158
Buhl, Marie-Louise (1918-) 781, 784, 798, 852, 854
Bundgaard, Jens Andersen (1897-1976) 302, 553, 554, 845
Bundgaard Rasmussen, Bodil (1947-) 945
Bülow-Jacobsen, Adam (1943-) 52, 151, 178, 179, 272, 323-348, 753, 782, 783, 786
Carlsen, Jesper (1957-) 439, 602, 614, 630, 779
Carra de Vaux, B. 115
Cataldi Dini, M. 649
Christensen, Johnny (1930-) 50, 201, 274, 1135
Christensen, Torben (1921-1983) 397, 419, 1110

Christiansen, Erik (1939-) 1005, 1008, 1015, 1024, 1040, 1046, 1050, 1051, 1054, 1058, 1062, 1063, 1075, 1181
Christiansen, Jette (1941-) 810, 817, 910, 915, 916, 936
Clausen, H.B. 612
Cochet, A. 697
Collin, Finn (1949-) 39
Cozza, L. 674
Dal, Erik (1922-) 781
Dalsgaard Larsen, Bent (1931-) 134-136, 1176
Damsgaard-Madsen, Aksel (1934-) 459, 520, 1181
Damsholt, Torben (1936-) 288
Daux, G. 606
Dietz, Søren (1940-) 443-446, 448-450, 455, 456, 609, 771, 773-775, 799, 800, 802, 902, 928, 973
Divari-Valakou, N. 455
Drachmann, Aage Gerhardt (1891-1980) 112, 115, 1160, 1161, 1163, 1164, 1169
Drukker, A. 904
Due, Bodil (1942-) 27, 95, 284-287
Due, Otto Steen (1939-) 143, 153-156, 190, 191, 202, 203, 278, 1176
Dybkjær Larsen, Jens (1950-) 617
Ebbesen, Sten (1946-) 42, 44, 46, 51, 52, 54-56, 111, 164, 188, 323, 1115-1120, 1122, 1133, 1134, 1136
el Sawy, S. 344
Engberg-Pedersen, Troels (1948-) 40, 41, 43, 47, 48, 270, 1099, 1137-1140
Esrom Larsen, Mogens (1942-) 1150
Fejfer, Jane (1955-) 739-741, 886, 889, 892, 898

Fine Licht, K. de – see: Licht, K.de F.
Finsen, Helge (1897-1976) 749
Fischer-Hansen, Tobias (1941-) 643, 646, 648-650, 653, 656, 657, 692, 793, 847, 903, 952, 1177, 1180
Fisker, Dorthe (1944-) 166
Foss, Otto (1902-1985) 1129
Fox, W.M 735
Friborg, Rud (1945-) 610a
Friedrich, Walter Ludwig (1938-) 610a, 612, 612a
Friis-Jensen, Karsten (1947-) 133, 192, 370, 371
Friis Johansen, Charlotte (1892-1973) 752
Friis Johansen, Holger (1927-1996) 7, 16, 21, 22, 24, 157, 163, 221, 222, 269, 388, 1176
Friis Johansen, Karsten (1930-) 184, 355, 1127
Fruelund Jensen, Børge (1947-) 145, 146
Gabrielsen, Vincent (1950-) 481, 504, 509, 512, 513, 521, 528, 529, 540, 549
Garcia-Diego, J.A. 1171
Gierow, P.G. 648
Ginge, Birgitte (1951-) 635-638, 684, 911, 925, 929, 930, 940-942, 946, 992
Giversen, Søren (1926-) 92, 161, 1093
Gjødesen, Mogens (1915-1989) 874
Godart, L. 969
Gradel, Ittai (1965-) 624
Gregory, T. 737
Grinder-Hansen, Keld (1956-) 407
Grønkjær, Niels (1955-) 398

Grønne, Claus (1957-) 678, 682, 687
Guldager, Pia (1961-) 676, 684, 737, 1080
Gundestrup, Bente (1946-) 1074
Hallager, Birgitte Pålsson (1948-) 291, 300, 583, 584, 587, 591, 597, 931
Hallager, Erik (1945-) 289-297, 299-301, 574-582, 585, 586, 588-590, 592-596, 801, 831, 926, 962-970, 1181
Hammer, Claus Uffe (1945-) 612
Hannestad, Lise (1943-) 765, 767, 768, 832, 901, 904, 917, 918, 922, 932, 938, 939, 943, 944, 951, 1099
Hannestad, Niels (1943-) 663, 738, 740, 822, 824, 825, 827, 871, 878, 879, 880, 890, 893, 894
Hansen, Erik (1927-) 604, 606, 608, 725, 732
Hansen, Jørgen (1947-) 685, 688, 697
Hansen, Jørgen Verner (1952-) 1095
Hansen, Mogens Herman (1940-) 45, 96, 274, 359, 460-467, 469-480, 482-502, 505, 506, 508, 510, 511, 514-519, 522-526, 530-539, 541-546, 550-552, 557, 561, 564
Hansen, Marianne V. (1954-) 503
Hansen, Ove (1955-) 28, 38, 76-79, 91, 150, 264, 271, 275, 276, 305-318, 360-362, 377, 404, 413, 451, 507, 547, 548, 571-573, 599, 601, 607, 611, 613, 1102
Hansen, Peter Allan (1944-) 13, 25, 26, 60-75, 80, 185, 186, 277, 303, 304, 562, 1175, 1179
Harding, Merete (1957-) 700, 701

Hastrup, Thure (1903-1989) 367a
Haugsted, Ida (1940-) 558
Hedeager, Lotte (1940-) 420
Heiberg, Johan Ludvig (1845-1928) 30, 101
Helbæk, Hans (1907-1981) 633
Hertz, Lotte Emilie (1963-) 691
Hill, D.R. 115
Hjortsø, Leo E. (1909-1996) 1132
Holck Kolding, Torben (1918-1998) 781
Holm-Nielsen, Svend (1919-) 751
Horsnæs, Helle W. (1961-) 625
Houby-Nielsen, Sanne (1960-) 421
Hude, Karl (1860-1936) 283
Hvidberg-Hansen, Finn O. (1935-) 756, 954
Hyldahl, Niels (1930-) 400
Hägg, I. 446
Hägg, R. 446
Højlund, Flemming (1943-) 713, 714
Høyrup, Jens (1943-) 1153-1156
Haarløv, Britt (1942-) 872, 873, 875, 881, 883, 891
Ingemann, Vibeke (1949-) 84
Isager, Jacob (1944-) 177, 180, 182, 417
Isager, Signe (1942-) 49, 142, 462, 702
Ishøj, H. – see: Smith, H.
Iversen, Erik (1909-2001) 1094
Jacobsen, Gurli (1957-) 700, 701
Jenkins, G.K. 1077
Jensen, Jørgen Steen. (1938-) 1055
Jensen, Marit (1955-) 738
Jensen, Povl Johs. (1911-1985) 1100, 1108, 1172
Jeppesen, Kristian (1924-) 158, 281,

282, 555, 559, 560, 565, 566, 705-710, 712, 713, 715, 717, 721, 769, 770, 933, 961, 974
Johansen, Flemming [Sidenius] (1934-) 860, 870, 876, 882, 884, 885, 887, 888, 900, 971, 980, 1083, 1177
Jorsal, Finn (1947-) 4, 33
Kiilerich, Bente (1954-) 567-569, 841, 855, 895, 896, 956, 957
Kill Jørgensen, Margit (1949-) 33
King, R.H. 735, 923
Kjeldsen, Kjeld (1943-) 724, 727
Kjærgaard, Jørgen (1957-) 672
Korsholm, Mette (1960-) 737
Kragelund, Patrick (1950-) 148, 160, 198, 217, 218, 279
Krarup, Per (1906-1977) 81, 87, 88, 369, 787
Kristensen, Anne K.G. (1927-) 249
Kromann (Balling), Anne (1936-1996) 772, 995, 1044, 1052, 1053, 1056, 1068-1070, 1075-1077, 1082
Kraay, C.M. 999, 1022
Larsen, Tage (1905-1975) 338
Larsen, Øjvind (1946-) 1123
Lauritsen, Jane (1945-) 379
Laursen, Simon (1958-) 86, 98, 99, 100
Lavrsen, Jytte (1929-1999) 693, 808
Le Roy, Chr. 725
Licht, Kjeld de Fine (1931-) 644, 645, 665, 666, 668, 669, 674, 679, 688
Lith, S.M.E. van 983
Liventhal, Viveca (1948-) 920
Lund, Allan A. (1944-) 58, 59, 83, 85, 90, 93, 149, 159, 208, 211, 213, 214, 224, 225, 227-235, 238, 239, 241-244, 246-248, 250-263, 265-268, 353, 391, 399, 438
Lund, Hakon (1928-) 664
Lund, John (1951-) 688, 736, 737, 744, 747, 762, 772, 776, 778, 792, 793, 803, 818, 934, 955, 958
Lund Hansen, Ulla (1942-) 988
Lundager Jensen, Hans Jørgen (1953-) 121
Luttrell, A. 717
Madvig, Johan Nicolai (1804-1886) 355, 1178
Malcus, Bengt (1933-) 424, 634
Markoulaki, S. 301
Mathiesen, Hans Erik (1949-1993) 739-741, 766, 1072, 1073
McCarren, V.P 339
Mejer, Jørgen (1942-) 14, 94, 97, 137, 169, 170, 358, 382, 383, 789, 1114, 1124-1126, 1128, 1141, 1173, 1174
Melander, Torben (1942-) 610, 936, 976, 990, 1091
Melis, F. 834
Meyer, Jørgen Christian (1950-) 405, 429, 667, 670
Mitchel, F. 501
Mitens, Karina (1954-) 829
Moesgaard, Kristian Peder (1939-) 195, 197, 1146, 1147, 1151
Moltesen, Mette (1944-) 658-660, 842, 843, 846, 849, 851, 861, 862, 865, 897, 899, 905, 935, 1080, 1088-1090
Motta, R. 674
Mougdad, S. 749
Mouritsen, Henrik (1962-) 622-624
Munk Olsen, Birger (1935-) 89, 394-396

Munksgaard, Elisabeth (1924-1997) 985
Mørch, Søren (1933-) 273
Mørkholm, Otto (1930-1983) 187, 442, 600, 994, 996-1004, 1006, 1007, 1009-1014, 1016-1023, 1025-1032, 1034-1039, 1041-1045, 1047-1049, 1064, 1076, 1078
Nedergaard, Elisabeth (1956-) 422, 680, 681
Neiiendam, Klaus (1938-) 619, 621
Neumann, G. 1011
Nielsen, Anne Marie (1949-) 856, 857, 912, 1086
Nielsen, Harald (1908-) 1157, 1159
Nielsen, Hanne Sigismund (1953-) 373, 374, 376, 378
Nielsen, Inge (1950-) 654, 662, 677, 678, 686, 689, 690, 751, 839, 840
Nielsen, Marjatta (1944-) 409, 411, 412, 414, 642, 793, 863, 864, 866-868, 1182
Nielsen, Palle Werner (1929-1991) 368
Nielsen, Thomas Heine (1963-) 508, 539, 541, 552
Nikolau, I. 1007
Nordquist, G. 928
Nylander, C. 675
Nøjgaard, Morten (1934-) 53, 380, 381, 384
Olçay, N. 997
Olivier, J.P. 598, 969
Ostenfeld, Erik Nis (1940-) 167, 168, 171-174, 1121, 1131
Pade, Marianne (1957-) 124
Panella, C. 674
Papachristodoulou, I. 443

Papanicolaou Christensen, Aristea (1936-) 563, 752, 754
Pavolini, C. 649, 653, 657, 833
Pedersen, Fritz Saaby (1945-) 319, 426
Pedersen, Lars (1959-) 545
Pedersen, Olaf (1920-1997) 181, 193, 1142, 1145
Pedersen, Poul (1947-) 703, 716, 718-720, 722, 723, 830
Pelon, O. 598
Peters, J. 283
Pietillä-Castrén, L. 654
Pihl, Mogens (1907-1986) 1142
Ploug, Gundhild (1937-) 745, 753, 754, 756, 758
Podemann Sørensen, Jørgen (1946-) 1096, 1097, 1113
Potts, Daniel (1953-) 763, 764, 832
Poulsen, Birte (1955-) 440, 602, 682
Poulsen, Erik (1945-) 777, 975, 977, 982, 993
Poulsen, Frederik (1876-1950) 603, 858, 859
Poulsen, Mark (1944-) 626
Poulsen, Vagn H. (1909-1971) 1083-1085
Poulsgaard Markussen, Erik (1951-) 627, 639-641, 790
Prytz Johansen, Jørgen (1911-1989) 1101
Pålsson, B. – see: Hallager, B.P.
Rafn, Birgitte (1939-1997) 447, 452, 457, 907, 947
Randsborg, Klavs (1944-) 403, 791, 828, 983
Rasmussen, Jens Elmegård (1944-) 364

Rathje, Annette (1942-) 410, 415, 416, 628, 651, 652, 655, 788, 792, 793, 806, 807, 809, 811-815, 819, 820, 833, 834, 869, 906, 914, 934, 979

Riis, Poul Jørgen (1910-) 742, 743, 746, 748, 755, 759-761, 816, 844, 853, 877, 953, 1080, 1081

Roberts, Helle Salskov (1933-) 805, 908, 909, 924, 948, 978, 981, 986, 987, 992a, 1071

Rubinstein, Lene (1964-) 508, 539, 541, 552

Rupp, D.W. 735, 736, 923

Raasted, Jørgen (1927-1995) 137, 1165

Salskov Roberts, H. – see: Roberts, H.S.

Sande, S. 683

Saxtorph, Niels M. (1923-2001) 436, 626

Schartau, Bjarne (1942-) 107, 354, 363

Schiøler, Thorkild (1927-) 661, 662, 671, 673, 750, 1162, 1166-1168, 1170, 1171

Schmidt, Olaf (1913-1996) 31

Scrinari, V.S.M. 647

Sigismund Nielsen, H. – see: Nielsen, H.S.

Skafte Jensen, Minna (1937-) 29, 119, 120, 122, 123, 125-129, 382, 383, 1105

Skouvig, Anders Chr. (1962-) 223

Skovgaard-Hansen, Michael (1945-) 216, 556

Skovgaard Jensen, Søren (1937-) 647, 1177

Skydsgaard, Jens Erik (1932-) 401, 402, 406, 430-432, 434, 527, 616, 618, 626, 1177

Slej, Karen (1956-) 676, 949

Smith, Hanne (1942-) 131, 199

Smith, Ole Langwitz (1943-1995) 1-3, 5, 6, 8-12, 15, 17-20, 23, 33-36, 106, 109, 113, 118, 130, 165, 200, 219, 220, 349-352, 354, 1183

Southworth, E. 892, 898

Stamatis, E.S. 30, 101

Strange, John (1934-) 794

Strøm, Ingrid (1929-) 408, 453, 454, 615, 629, 631, 796, 797, 804, 913, 984, 989, 991

Styrenius, C.-G. 445, 446, 579, 581

Søby Christensen, Arne (1945-) 147

Sørensen, Lone Wriedt (1948-) 734-737, 803, 848, 850, 919, 923, 927, 937, 950, 959

Sørensen, Søren (1954-) 132

Sørensen, Villy (1945-2001) 205-207, 1103, 1104, 1106

Saaby Pedersen, F. – see: Pedersen, F.S.

Taisbak, Christian Marinus (1934-) 102-105, 114, 189, 194, 1148, 1149

Tauber, Henrik (1921-) 610a, 612, 612a

Thierfelder, A. 175

Thompson, M. 999, 1022

Thomsen, Marie-Louise (1950-) 385

Thomsen, Ole (1946-) 32, 37, 204

Thomsen, Rudi (1918-) 425, 427, 441, 458, 468, 754, 1066, 1067

Torp, H. 896, 956

Torresin, Giuseppe (1924-) 176

Tortzen, Christian Gorm (1951-) 366

Trolle, Steffen (1942-) 771, 772, 795
Tschäpe, R. 862
Tvarnø, Henrik (1954-) 437, 779
Tzedakis, Y. 580, 582, 585, 586, 588, 589, 593, 595, 966
Ussing, Johan Louis (1820-1905) 175
Vanggaard, Jens H. (1941-) 1107, 1109, 1111
Vestergaard, Torben (1964-) 508, 539, 541, 552
Vlasakis, M. 293, 299-301, 595, 596, 962
Wagner, Peter Henrik (1942-) 612a
Wanscher, Ole (1903-1985) 433
Weber-Lehmann, C. 1090
Whitehorne, J.E.G. 333
Whittle, E.W. 21, 22
Wiese, Conrad Frederik (1896-1967) 367
Wikander, Ö. 671
Wild, J.P. 826
Wriedt Sørensen, L. – see: Sørensen, L.W.
Zahle, Jan (1942-) 675, 677, 683, 704, 705, 707, 711, 724, 726-731, 733, 1000, 1009, 1033, 1057, 1059-1061, 1099
Zerner, C. 928
Zevi, F. 646, 648
Ørsted, Peter (1942-) 423, 428, 695, 780
Østergaard, Jan Stubbe (1948-) 696, 960, 1087
Aaboe, Asger (1922-) 1144
Aaris-Sørensen, Kim (1946-) 713

Danish Humanist Texts and Studies

Edited for the Royal Library by Erland Kolding Nielsen

Volume 1
Peter Allan Hansen:
Bibliography of Danish Contributions to Classical Scholarship from the Sixteenth Century to 1970.
1977. 335 pages. Cloth.

Volume 2
Stephanus Johannis Stephanius:
Notæ Uberiores in Historiam Danicam Saxonis Grammatici. Sorø 1645.
Facsimile edition with an introduction by H. D. Schepelern.
1978. 362 pages. Cloth.

Volume 3
Hanne Trautner-Kromann:
Skjold og sværd. Jødisk polemik mod kristendommen og de kristne i Frankrig og Spanien fra 1100-1500. [Dissertation]
1990. 236 pages. Out of print.

Volume 4
Birgit Bjørnum & Klaus Møllerhøj:
Carl Nielsens Samling. Katalog over komponistens musikhåndskrifter i Det kongelige Bibliotek. / The Carl Nielsen Collection. A Catalogue of the Composers Musical Manuscripts in the Royal Library.
1992. 275 pages. Illustrated. Cloth.

Volume 5
Harald Ilsøe:
Bogtrykkerne i København og deres virksomhed ca. 1600-1810.
En biobibliografisk håndbog med bidrag til bogproduktionens historie.
Mit deutscher Zusammenfassung.
1992. 307 pages. Illustrated. Cloth.

Volume 6
Kirsten Dreyer (ed.):
Kamma Rahbeks brevveksling med Chr. Molbech.
With an Introduction and Notes by Kirsten Dreyer.
1993-94. 940 pages, 3 volumes. Illustrated. Cloth.

Volume 7
Ruth Bentzen (ed.):
Ung sprogforsker på rejse. Breve fra og til Holger Pedersen 1892-1896.
With an Introduction and Notes by Ruth Bentzen.
1994. 285 pages. Cloth.

Volume 8
Flemming Gorm Andersen:
Danmark og Antikken 1980-1991. En bibliografi over 12 års dansksproget litteratur om den klassiske oldtid.
1994. 308 pages. Cloth.

Volume 9
Bjarne Schartau:
Codices Graeci Haunienses. Ein deskriptiver Katalog des griechischen Handschriftenbestandes der königlichen Bibliothek Kopenhagen.
1994. 615 pages + 40 plates. Illustrated. Cloth.

Volume 10
Dan Fog:
Lumbye-Katalog. Fortegnelse over H. C. Lumbyes trykte kompositioner. Verzeichnis der gedruckten Kompositionen von H.C. Lumbye (1810-74).
1995. 176 pages. Illustrated.

Volume 11
Grethe Jacobsen:
Kvinder, køn og købstadslovgivning 1400-1600. Lovfaste mænd og ærlige kvinder.
Mit deutscher Zusammenfassung. [Habilitationsschrift]
1995. 387 pages. Cloth.

Volume 12
Birgitte Possing & Bruno Svindborg (eds.):
Det Kongelige Biblioteks Håndskriftafdeling: Erhvervelser 1924-1987. Vejledning i benyttelse. / The Royal Library, The Manuscript Department: Acquisitions 1924-1987. Guide for Users.
1995. 675 pages, 2 volumes. Cloth.

Volume 13
Carol Gold:
Educating Middle Class Daughters.
Private Girls Schools in Copenhagen 1790-1820.
1996. 244 pages. Illustrated. Cloth.

Volume 14
Paul Flandrup & Kristine Heltberg (eds.):
C.W. Smith i jego polscy korespondenci / C.W. Smith og hans polske korrespondenter 1861-1879. A correspondence published with a Danish translation, introduction and notes.
With English Summary.
1997. 371 pages. Illustrated. Cloth.

Volume 15
Michael Bregnsbo:
Samfundsorden og statsmagt set fra prædikestolen.
Danske præsters deltagelse i den offentlige opinionsdannelse vedrørende samfundsordenen og statsmagten 1750-1848 belyst ved trykte prædikener.
With an English Summary.
1997. 464 pages, Illustrated. Cloth.

Volume 16
Henrik Horstbøll & John T. Lauridsen (eds.):
Den trykte kulturarv. Pligtaflevering gennem 300 år.
With an English Summary.
1998. 631 pages. Illustrated. Cloth.

Volume 17
Inger Sørensen (ed.):
J.P.E. Hartmann og hans kreds. En komponistfamilies breve 1780-1900.
1999 (vol. 1-3) & 2002 (vol. 4). 2460 pages, 4 volumes. Illustrated. Cloth.

Volume 18
Erik Petersen:
Intellectum liberare. Johann Albert Fabricius - en humanist i Europa.
Mit deutscher Zusammenfassung. [Habilitationsschrift].
1998. 1090 pages, 2 volumes. Illustrated. Cloth.

Volume 19
Henrik Horstbøll:
Menigmands medie. Det folkelige bogtryk i Danmark 1500-1840. En kulturhistorisk undersøgelse.
With an English Summary. [Dissertation]
1999. 795 pages. Illustrated. Cloth.

Volume 20
John T. Lauridsen:
Krig, købmænd og kongemagt – og andre 1600-tals studier.
1999. 333 pages.

Volume 21
Harald Ilsøe:
Det Kongelige Bibliotek i støbeskeen: Studier og samlinger til bestandens historie indtil ca. 1780.
With an English Summary.
1999. 717 pages, 2 volumes. Illustrated. Cloth.

Volume 22
Søren Gosvig Olesen:
Transcendental historie: Overvejelser angående den menneskelige erkendelse.
2000. 112 pages. Cloth.

Volume 23
Charlotte Appel:
Læsning og bogmarked i 1600-tallets Danmark.
With an English Summary. [Dissertation]
2001. 1009 pages, 2 volumes. Illustrated. Cloth.

Volume 24
John T. Lauridsen:
Samarbejde og modstand. Danmark under den tyske besættelse 1940-45.
En bibliografi.
With an Introduction in English.
2002. 687 pages. Cloth.

Volume 25
Claus Røllum-Larsen:
Impulser i Københavns koncertrepertoire 1900-1935: Studier i præsentationen af ny, især udenlandsk instrumentalmusik.
With an English Summary.
2002. 310 + 382 pages, 2 volumes. Illustrated. Cloth.

Volume 26
John T. Lauridsen:
„Føreren har ordet!" - Frits Clausen om sig selv og DNSAP.
2003. 846 pages. Illustrated. Cloth

Volume 27
Flemming Gorm Andersen:
Danish Contributions to Classical Scholarship 1971-1991. A Bibliography.
2004. 160 pages. Cloth.

Volume 28
Mads Mordhorst & Jes Fabricius Møller:
Historikeren Caspar Paludan-Müller.
April 2004. c. 350 pages. Illustrated. Cloth.

Volume 29
Olav Harsløf (ed.):
Georg Brandes og Europa.
April 2004. c. 425 pages + DVD, "Georg Brandes i Firenze". Illustrated.

All books can be obtained from bookshops, The Museum Tusculanum Press or on the internet.

Museum Tusculanum Press
Njalsgade 94
DK-2300 Copenhagen S
Denmark

Homepage: www.mtp.dk